THROUGH THE
EYES OF
JESUS

Coming to Appreciate Jesus More Fully

DR. WILLIAM L. STEPHENS

THROUGH THE EYES OF JESUS
Copyright ©2025 Dr. William L. Stephens

978-1-998815-34-0 Soft Cover
978-1-998815-35-7 E-book

Printed in Canada and the USA

Published by:
Castle Quay Books
Little Britain, Ontario, Canada
Jupiter, Florida, USA
Tel: (416) 573-3249
E-mail: info@castlequaybooks.com | www.castlequaybooks.com

Edited by Marina Hofman Willard PhD
Cover design and book interior by Burst Impressions

For Library of Congress Cataloging Information please contact the publisher.

For Library and Archives Canada Cataloguing in Publication Information please contact the publisher.

CASTLE QUAY BOOKS

CHAPTER ONE

MISPLACED APPRECIATION

Suddenly, I hear a loud, powerful voice that calls out my name—"Bill!" I turn quickly to see where it's coming from, but my front yard is empty. It is kinda dark, so someone could be hiding nearby. I turn around a few times. I search every hiding place but find nothing. The voice repeats my name—it sounds right next to me but can't be! Maybe it's my friends playing a joke on me—and I do admit this is a pretty good one.

I yell, "Come on, guys, cut it out! It's not funny anymore!" I am confused but not scared.

Then I hear the voice say clearly, "Bill, do not be afraid; I will not hurt you. I love you."

———————

Today, something a little different happened in my routine. I was about to get into my car at the supermarket when a bag boy came running out to ask if the bag he was holding was mine. Embarrassed but appreciative, I told him that, yes, indeed, it is mine. I then quickly checked my man-bag to be sure everything else was still accounted for.

I joked with the boy about my creeping senility at such a young age and offered him a nice tip. "Thank you, but no, sir, that's just part of our service." I thanked him in return.

On the way home, I smiled as I thought about that bag boy. I reminded myself that others like me still do such unselfish acts. Like letting a cashier know that I've been undercharged. Returning lost items to their rightful owners and stopping to help a stranded motorist.

I often wonder why more people aren't like me and that bag boy.

I am reminded, to my annoyance, that few people thank me for my honesty and selflessness like the bag boy. Not being appreciated irritates me. I know I don't need to be thanked for everything nice I do. I just want to be appreciated a little bit more. Not that you always need to be thanked, but it is nice sometimes. I feel good about being appreciated. I take great pride in my humility.

I got home and started to take my groceries into the house. My wife was out of town, so for a few days, I had to cope for myself.

That's when I heard the voice.

Initially, I did not respond but thought, *It can't be! How could it be?* And finally, *It must be!* I then struggled to say quite shyly, "Are you God?"

And I sensed God Himself answer, "Yes, Bill, of course I am! Could we go inside and talk?'

I nodded yes, and we went inside. We were alone. I stood there, shaking. Not knowing what to say, I sat down. And I thought, *Is God really sitting … standing in my living room? Why?*

God said, "Don't be nervous or afraid; please sit down." God smiled (I could hear it in His voice) and then continued, "Let's get down to business. I've been watching you and listening to you for quite a while. I believe you have a great deal of spiritual potential. But you also have a lot of weak spots I want to talk to you about. Starting tonight, if you are willing."

Whatever You say, God! I am ready! I think.

God smiled again and said, "Where to start? … Let's take today. I was looking at everything you did, said, and thought about the events you experienced. I assume it was a somewhat typical day until, of course, the last few minutes. The topics of pride and appreciation came up quite a lot. It is interesting how you expended too much time on one of these topics and way too little on the other. Let Me elaborate.

"You do many wonderful things in your life that benefit many people who need help. But—and this is very important—who are you doing it for? Is it for Me? Or is it for you? A few minutes ago, you made a few unacceptable statements for a 'strong' Christian to believe or make. One was 'All of this makes me feel good about myself,' and the other was 'I take great pride in my humility.'"

God continued, chastising me for being a prideful person more impressed with myself than Him. He told me that, more often than not, I do nice things mainly for recognition and appreciation! Then He made it quite clear that He does not appreciate my attitude of self-satisfaction and pride.

In a softened voice, God reminded me that many of my perceived self-less acts of kindness are selfish and prideful! He pointed out, "Don't you usually expect to be thanked? Don't you always desire recognition? Don't you always want to be appreciated?" He made it clear that many of my "acts of love" in no way reflect the unconditional love that He provides. My love is usually entirely conditional, depending on the recipient's expression of thanks and appreciation.

By now, I was wondering if agreeing to have this conversation was wise. I thought, *How long is this going to go on?* But then, realizing that God could read my thoughts, I thought, *Oops, sorry, God, I forgot You were listening … Please go on!*

God continued. "You expect to be appreciated for all your minor acts of kindness, which you seem to believe are many. Trust Me, I've kept track of them, and you still have plenty of hands to count on. Also, you treat these few actions as if they represent the ultimate acts of unselfishness or unconditional love. Think again! You even expect to be appreciated for simply being 'appreciative' of others. But what about Me? What about My Son, Jesus? What about all We have done for you? Do you appreciate Us? Tell me exactly, how do you demonstrate your appreciation to Us?"

Without thinking, I immediately and foolishly responded with, "Of course, I appreciate you, Lord," to which God let me know my response was way too quick, weak, and insincere. I thought, *Bill, just stop opening your mouth!*

"All right," said God. "Let's just see how much you appreciate Me. You might want to take notes." I said nothing, wishing I had remained silent the first time. Then God reached into something invisible and handed me a notebook to work on. Boy, was I glad I had not pointed out to God that I had nothing to write on ... or with. He then gave me a pen. I first wrote, "Never respond out loud unless God asks me a question. Even then, don't respond too quickly." I then waited for God to begin.

God reminded me that I like to show appreciation for the kind acts of others. "You thank another shopper if he lets you get in front of him in line. You then pass along this kindness by letting another shopper get in front of you, and then you feel smug for having done it."

God continued: "You finally have longtime neighbors come over for dinner for the first time, in appreciation for their bringing you chicken soup every day you were sick in bed and for going to the pharmacy to pick up your many prescriptions."

"Yes," I said sheepishly. "I can be very appreciative. Not everyone would do what I did." I quickly realized the stupidity of that last statement and said, "Sorry, God! At least I'm beginning to catch on to what You are talking about before You even have to point it out. Does that count for anything?"

I thought I heard God take a frustrated sigh before responding, "It could have if you hadn't also asked Me to give you credit for it."

He continued, probing me much more deeply. "Since you accepted My Son as your Savior, how much change has occurred in your life? Whom have you told about My gift of salvation? How often have you thanked Me for having sent Jesus to you? How often have you thanked Jesus for obediently following My will and coming to earth?"

God, on a roll, went on. "When you attended your mother's funeral, you casually commented that at least she's no longer in pain. And that she is in a far better place. Did these common clichés bring a torrent of joyful tears to you as you understood the significance of her spending eternity in heaven rather than in hell and free from all pain? Did you ever say in appreciation and with all reverence, 'Thank You, Jesus'?"

I decided not to respond. But God did. He said: "I don't remember hearing you say any of that."

God went on. "Think about when your unsaved brother died. Did the realization that he would spend eternity in hell bring a flood of tears of sorrow to you? It should have. Did the fact that you never shared your faith with him make you fall to your knees in guilt and sadness? It should have. Did you say, 'Forgive me, Jesus'? Did you promise to share your faith with your other unsaved relatives? Have you followed through on that promise?"

God asked me to consider further: "How do you react to what Jesus had to endure for you in Pilate's torture chamber when whips of stone, glass, and bone tore apart His body? When He suffered from rejections, betrayals, denials, and the very weight of the cross on His back by those closest to Him on the road to Golgotha? When you imagine the pain and suffering He must have felt when the crown of thorns was forced onto His head and when His hands and feet were nailed to the cross?

"What do you feel when you think about the emotional oppression that My Son, Jesus, who was completely untouched and unstained with sin until that very moment, had to endure when He was exposed to the entirety of the sins of all humanity? Do these thoughts have any impact on you? Does your heart ache for Jesus? Or are you able to simply shrug it off? Don't you ever show any evidence of genuine appreciation?"

God then changed His line of questioning. "How about when you are alone on a gloriously clear night when a brilliant full moon and millions of stars light the cloudless darkness? There is nothing but you and the wonder of nature—My creation—around you. Are you ever dumbstruck? Unable to speak when it dawns on you that I created all this beauty for you to enjoy? Do you ever say, 'Wow!' and stop to give Me praise for My love, creativity, vastness, and beauty?

"When your little girl was born, did you stop to think about the miracle of her life that only I could create? I knew of your precious creation long before I knitted her in the womb. Did you ever express awe? Did you think about other miracles of life that were never born because they were destroyed during abortion? Did you consider the anguish of many women who later realized what they did? Did you every grieve for them?"

I was stunned by these questions! Speechless! It was tough even to swallow. As I was forced to think of answers to these questions, I became sad and depressed. I could not think of a single acceptable answer. Had I ever understood the significance of what Jesus has done for me, for all humanity? No, I had not! Had I ever adequately shown my appreciation to Jesus? I am sure I had not. I had simply taken it all for granted, and I still do. And I am deeply disappointed in myself for my ingratitude.

I realized that I am not even sure what "appreciation" means regarding God. Words seem so inadequate to describe what my reactions and responses should be. Dictionary definitions of being grateful or thankful are not even close to what I should feel. The emotions of valuing highly or holding in awe are at least getting closer. When I consider concepts such as to treasure, to regard as precious, or to cherish, the words seem to have an honest and powerful meaning—to me, at least.

Using these concepts, I tried to evaluate my appreciation of Jesus. Can I truthfully say that I treat my relationship with Him as precious? Do I cherish Him? Do I treasure His greatest commandment, to "love the Lord with all my heart, all my soul, all my strength and all my being"? Answering honestly, I realize that I have hardly ever come close to appreciating Jesus in this manner.

I was found guilty of not appreciating Jesus as I should, so I asked myself, "How can I change all that? How can I come to treasure, cherish, and hold precious all that Jesus has done, continues to do, and will always do for me? I must try. But how? I need guidance, direction, wisdom, discernment, and enlightenment."

God told me, "I have an idea, which you will consider quite unusual. It involves what I consider to be quite sincere concerns on your part. Before you go to sleep tonight, I want you to let Me know if you want to go on a long journey back in time, where you can see things firsthand and find out exactly how appreciative you are of My Son. It will take a week of our time, requiring the greatest emotional swings you will ever experience. You may or may not be the same person when you return. Your reactions will be entirely based on the depths of your faith.

"No more questions for now, Bill! I will get back to you before you go to sleep tonight, and I expect a decision from you then."

CHAPTER TWO

MY SEARCH FOR GUIDANCE

T hat night, I spent much time in prayer, aware of everything God had chastised me for. Every bit of it was valid, and I was sincerely embarrassed and ashamed. I had disappointed God so many times, making promises I usually broke. What could I do that would prove my willingness to risk it all? Of course, I realized that risking it could mean being willing to give up my life for Jesus. I have been thinking a lot lately about this very issue. Here in America, the odds are minimal that standing up for our faith can result in losing our lives. But what if I went on a mission trip to Iran or Malaysia with an organization like Open Doors, which involves bringing Bibles and cash into the country to distribute to Christian organizations?

Although the odds of being caught and put to death are small, there are many stories of missionaries at least being incarcerated and tortured—all in the name of Jesus. It bothers me that I have been unwilling to make such a trip—simply because I fear the possible consequences of death or severe persecution.

I then went to God's book. I needed to know if the Bible says anything about avoiding situations where one must die to stand with Jesus. If we were unwilling, would it mean we would go to hell instead? What if we never committed to Jesus to give up our life for Him but never faced the actual decision? What then? I reviewed the most familiar verses on how we can be saved, and they don't seem to imply anything about dying for Jesus.

"Believe in the Lord Jesus, and you will be saved—you
and your household." (Acts 16:31)

God so loved the world that he gave his one and only Son,
that whoever believes in him shall not perish but have
eternal life. (John 3:16)

In these verses and numerous others, I found no reference to the issue
of dying for Jesus. I've also been to many churches during their altar calls.
Not once do I remember the invitation, including the qualification of being
willing to lose our lives for Jesus. I never remember any discussions in
church as to whether salvation may require literal death. I'm confused.

God responded, "These are indeed wonderful verses that are very
popular. However, others must be considered as well. Now tell me what
you think."

Do not be afraid of what you are about to suffer. I tell
you, the devil will put some of you in prison to test you,
and you will suffer persecution for ten days. Be faithful,
even to the point of death, and I will give you life as your
victor's crown. (Revelation 2:10)

Whoever does not take up their cross and follow me is not
worthy of me. Whoever finds their life will lose it, and
whoever loses their life for my sake will find it. (Matthew
10:38–39)

God then gave me one more verse to consider. It relates to persecution
during the end times. Matthew 24 says:

"Nation will rise against nation and kingdom against kingdom. There will be famines and earthquakes in various
places. All these are the beginning of birth pains.

"Then you will be handed over to be persecuted and put to death, and you will be hated by all nations because of me." (Matthew 24:7–9)

God asked me, "What do you think?"

I responded, "Sure seems pretty clear to me. A lot of people who claim to be Christians are going to be surprised one day! ... God, I want You to know that I've made a decision ... I will be honored to give my life for You if the time ever comes."

God responded, "Indeed, you are correct about surprises. I am also proud of you, and I knew you would also make the decision you have. I just wanted to hear you say it. That is why I am giving you the option I mentioned a little while ago. And to remind you, there will be no further questions or explanations on my part except this. I will also be where you are going. You will not be alone."

No longer nervous, I said without pausing, "I can't wait to go."

"I also look forward to being with you. Have a good rest; you'll need it."

"Excuse me. One last question—if it's OK?" I sheepishly asked.

"Sure. One more."

"I know without a doubt that You are indeed God. But to which of You three am I now talking?" I asked. "And by what name do I call You?"

"Bill, that is an excellent question that can have a complex answer. But let's keep it simple. If you simply call me God, I will call you Bill. How's that?"

"Wonderful! Thank you."

CHAPTER THREE

MY STRANGE NEW WORLD

I soon fell asleep after telling God of my willingness to go out on a spiritual limb, and I awoke refreshed with a calm spirit of renewed hope. It was strange but wonderful, as if something mystical was about to happen. When I opened my eyes, everything seemed foreign. I recognized nothing—not my room, not my surroundings. At first, I concluded it was simply a dream and that I should go with the flow and enjoy the ride of excitement.

But something was different about this "dream." It wasn't a dream! It seemed to be honest! But how could it be?

Where am I? It seems to be in a third-world country!

I was no longer in my Sleep Number bed. Instead, I felt the prickly points of straw laid out on a makeshift mat on a dirt floor. I was not physically uncomfortable. And even more surprisingly, I was not emotionally uncomfortable. I was pretty calm. Curious, yes, but not scared or worried.

I looked out the open window of this mud dwelling and saw some twenty to thirty people already busy. They smiled and waved to me occasionally and even said a few words that I was too far away to hear. They seemed to know me—but why? How could they? I had never been here before. I had never met them. But they were so friendly, and their gaze was respectful, almost adoring.

That made me feel quite uncomfortable. What was going on? Who did they think I was?

I called out to them. No response! I tried again, even louder. Still no reaction! Like they did not hear me. I could listen to myself speak, but they apparently could not. I was so confused.

Despite my sense that it was real, my mind said it must be a dream I hoped I would remember when I woke up and could analyze. My concern was that it would be like most of my other dreams—they'd make complete sense while I was asleep but be quickly forgotten or irrational once I awoke.

Then came a voice. A very quiet voice. At first, I thought it had to be God the Father. He said He'd be here. But it sounded different.

This new voice was quite near. It spoke to me: "Bill, this is not a dream. It is more real than anything you have ever experienced. Your prayer is being answered. You asked My Father to be able to understand better what I suffered for you. Surprisingly, very few people ask this favor or even care. You asked to see what I saw. Feel how I felt. Walk with Me and observe My world through My own eyes."

I could not hold it in. It was impossible. It couldn't be Him. "Pardon me for interrupting. I do seem to have a bad habit of it, but You just mentioned talking to Your Father. You also said You have suffered for me. So that could only mean I must be talking now to God's Son Jesus in the flesh? Am I correct?"

"Yes, it is I! And My Father is also with Me. And you will be with Us both for the next full week. You will be experiencing everything I experience."

I was stunned. As I usually do, I spoke up. "Why me? I am not deserving of this. Your Father must have told You how weak my faith is and how little I have done for You. And of my lack of proper respect and appreciation for who You are, all You have done and will do for me."

Jesus answered, "Bill, since I live in you, and you live in Me, we are one body in the Spirit. For that reason, and because you asked, from this moment on this week, I will allow you to experience everything I experience except the full extent of the physical pain I will have to endure. Everything I see, you will see. Whatever you feel will be both your feelings and Mine. Join Me for the last days of My life. And when this short journey is over, write down what you remember, and share it with others so they can better understand how much I love them."

Jesus continued, "There are just a few rules. First, this will be the last time you will talk directly with Me. From now on, your communication will only be with My Father. I will be quite busy talking to My disciples, the crowds, the religious leaders, the pilgrims, and My Father. You also will be unable to converse with any of My followers. You will be able to understand everything that is said, but you cannot respond. And of course, My Father will always be nearby for you."

I was stunned! I was in awe. I was speechless. The answer to my prayer would be far greater than I could ever imagine. Amazingly, I had complete peace. Why not? Jesus's Spirit indwelled me. And I would soon be walking with Him—as a part of Him during the last few days of His life on earth.

I turned to God the Father, only guessing where He was in the room. "I don't know what to say. This is the most unbelievable, astounding thing that has happened in my life. Thank You so much for this opportunity to be here in Your presence. As You always are, of course. I know You are always with me no matter where I am!"

God responded, "Yes, I am always there for you. I know everything you will say as soon as you think about saying it. But I usually wait until after you speak to respond. I want to give you a chance to change your mind since your thoughts are not always godly."

I responded sheepishly, "Got it! I'll work harder on my initial thoughts … very carefully."

CHAPTER FOUR

THE RAISING OF LAZARUS

Time passed quickly, as if a fast-forward button had been pressed on Jesus's life DVR machine. Events I had only read about in the Bible were happening firsthand. We were less than one week before Jesus's death. Passover was fast approaching, and people everywhere were buzzing. I could sense that wherever we went. It was shortly after Jesus raised His good friend Lazarus from the dead. Everyone wanted to see the Man who had performed this and many other miracles. We were now on our way to Jerusalem to celebrate the Passover, just as Jesus had done every year since He was twelve years old.

There was a disturbing sense that something was about to happen—something ominous—as tension was heavy in the air. Word was circulating that the Pharisees and other leaders were plotting to have Jesus arrested and killed if and when He entered the city of Jerusalem. Many in the crowds were encouraging Jesus to go to Jerusalem, some probably hoping that this troublemaker would be arrested; others expecting that if He were indeed the promised Messiah, then maybe He would finally identify himself as the Messiah and free the Jews from their Roman oppression. Many of Jesus's closest friends pleaded with Him not to go, fearing for His safety. After all, He had offended many people in positions of power. And the buzz on the street was that anyone who knew of Jesus's plans should report them to the Pharisees. Rumors also included financial rewards being offered for such information.

This commotion had convinced Jesus to cut back on His public appearances. I sensed that He was concerned about what the emotional and sometimes irrational crowds might do if He stayed in the public eye. I could also tell by His apparent fatigue that Jesus needed rest. Jesus's tranquil spirit assured me that His withdrawal to a quiet place was not based on any sense of fear He might have had—the type that many of His followers demonstrated. It seemed instead that Jesus was biding His time in a calculated manner as if He was waiting for just the right moment to do something meaningful.

Yes, I sensed that Jesus was completely relaxed and at peace. At least for now, we were all calm. We waited. During rest, my mind wandered, and God often responded to these mere thoughts. I thought of a pun, as I am prone to, and then tried to replace it with something "more appropriate immediately." People always tell me that puns are the lowest form of humor. I hope God had not noticed because I had no idea what God thought of my sense of humor.

Without my asking God, He responded, "I know exactly what you are thinking. And I am glad you almost asked me for clarity. I knew that sooner or later, this would have to come up if we worked together like we now do. I have a very low opinion of humor and puns in particular. I was going to discuss this before I decided to give you this opportunity, but somehow, I forgot."

God told me this, all while smiling. I took a real risk by what I said next. And if I was wrong, I would be in deep trouble. I said, "Wait a minute, You said You forgot to talk to me about it. But You are God. You cannot forget! What's up?"

God chuckled and then said. "Very good! Most impressive. You're not intimidated enough to accept my comment as is. It takes spunk to say that. And I am so pleased that we are comfortable enough with each other to do so. You know, I enjoyed including a sense of humor in human personalities. I wanted humanity to enjoy humor. I want humor and laughter to be expressions of delight and joy. And that is why I gave you a great sense of humor, especially your puns. Not everyone has the instincts needed for puns.

"But remember, almost all things in life require moderation. Very few things are ever good in excess. So here are some quick rules you can use at a minimum. Never intend to hurt others or offend Me; never decide on what is acceptable humor when drinking; and remember, I am always in your audience."

I thanked God and carefully considered God's advice for the next few minutes.

Later that day, I thought about our time in Ephraim a few days ago. We had traveled to Ephraim, close to the wilderness where Jesus had once spent forty days resisting Satan. The serenity of this place gave us all plenty of time to reflect, pray, and prepare. Indeed, I needed more time to think about where we had just come from, Bethany, where I felt confused.

I have to admit that raising Lazarus was somewhat confusing to me. I did not completely understand the emotions I felt then—the emotions that came to me from Jesus. I was surprised that Jesus had wept when He learned from Mary that Lazarus had died.

It made sense that losing His friend would sadden Jesus since Jesus was fully man. And yet, since Jesus was fully God, He must have known in advance that He would raise Lazarus from the dead. So why would His response be that of sadness? As I reflected further on this, I came to believe that Jesus's response may have had less to do with the death of Lazarus than it had to do with everyone's reaction to the death of Lazarus. Mary and Martha expressed their faith in Jesus when they came to Him and said, "If you had been here, my brother would not have died." They did indeed believe that Jesus could have healed their brother right up to the point of death. But hadn't they expressed a lack of faith in Jesus by not even considering the possibility that Jesus could triumph over death, and not just sickness?

I asked God to help me understand. He said, "You are correct that Mary and Martha had observed Jesus healing people, but they had never seen Him raise anyone from the grave. So far, their faith had been limited to only what they had seen, observed, and experienced. Although Mary and Martha were two of Jesus's closest friends, they had little idea of exactly who Jesus was and what He could and would do for them and others. That was not what saddened Jesus. Other things were going on as well."

I then remembered something else. When Lazarus first came out of the burial cave, I noticed a renewed sense of belief on the part of many onlookers. But I also felt a sense of disappointment in Jesus. Again, I wondered why.

I wondered, "Was Jesus disappointed in the lack of depth in the onlookers' renewed faith? A faith that He knew would be temporary, shallow, and fleeting. A faith completely conditional on miraculous events that showed the power of Jesus. A belief that would be quickly forgotten once the miracles were no longer a daily occurrence."

God responded by nodding in agreement.

From my unique vantage point through the eyes of Jesus, I saw that many of the onlookers were talking with the Pharisees, as spies or reporters might do. I did not know if the Pharisees had sent these onlookers, but I could tell that they were both interested and disturbed by the news that was brought to them. They often engaged in heated debates afterward. Perhaps this is what had disappointed Jesus.

God again agreed with my assessment.

My memory returned to the great banquet that celebrated this miracle. Many of the people who came were Lazarus's good friends, joyful that he was alive, and wanting to offer him well wishes and love. Others there were skeptics. They came to assure themselves that the man who left the cave was not an imposter and that a miracle had occurred.

Judas was here and made his presence known in a way consistent with the reputation that preceded Him. Rumors had been circulating that Judas was using his position as treasurer of the disciples for his gain. His response at the banquet to a spontaneous act of love for Jesus lent credibility to the rumors. One of Jesus's followers had anointed Jesus's feet with expensive perfume, and the aroma filled the air with a wonderful fragrance that everyone seemed to enjoy. Everyone, that is, except Judas. He expressed his opposition based on his pretense of concern for the poor. He argued that selling the perfume could have raised money to minister to their needs rather than see it wasted in this frivolous manner.

God said, "Very good. You are getting quite perspective in your assessments. Keep it up!"

Looking at Judas through Jesus's eyes, it was painfully obvious how insincere Judas appeared to be. We could tell that every time an ounce of perfume landed on Jesus's feet, a cringe of agony swept across Judas's face as he saw the potential money being soaked up by the dirt floor.

As hard as I tried, I was surprised that I could not look at Judas with contempt and disdain. I think I could not because Jesus did not. Jesus's reaction was not of surprise, anger, or even disappointment. It was more of a quiet resignation, as if Jesus were saying, "I know. I know."

God said, "When you get home, try being this understanding and forgiving more often."

I then came back from my recollection of Bethany to the present. Jesus announced it was time to leave the peacefulness of the wilderness and begin the last leg of His final trip to Jerusalem. We came very close to the Mount of Olives as we traveled through Bethphage. I wondered why Jesus had stopped and gazed into the garden for such a long time, not remembering at that moment that it would later have such great significance for all of us.

CHAPTER FIVE
ON TO JERUSALEM!

As we neared Jerusalem, the crowds had grown quite large and appeared at first to be entirely in support of Jesus. I heard Jesus ask two disciples to look for a colt and a donkey. When they found them, the disciples were to untie them and bring them to Jesus, for it had been prophesied that Jesus would enter Jerusalem on a donkey and even a colt. The disciples did as asked and soon returned with the two animals. Clothes were placed on their backs, and Jesus mounted the colt for the ride into the city. It was a ride that history would later describe as the triumphant entry of Jesus.

The crowds became electric. Thousands upon thousands of people spread their coats and leafy branches onto the road as they loudly proclaimed,

> "Hosanna! Blessed is he who comes in the name of the Lord! Blessed is the coming kingdom of our father David! Hosanna in the highest heaven!" (Mark 11:9–10)

We also heard repeatedly,

> "Blessed is the king who comes in the name of the Lord! Peace in heaven and glory in the highest!" (Luke 19:38)

Amid this celebration, a very strange set of emotions came over me. It was hardly what I expected. Surprisingly, only a tiny part of what I felt was happiness, enthusiasm, and joy on such a joyous occasion. I had a much greater sense of somberness, with sober acceptance of what was to happen. I knew this was how I felt because it was what Jesus felt, and I wondered why.

I tried to understand more of what was going on in the crowd, what Jesus had been understanding all along, but I seemed to be missing. I needed to focus with greater concentration so as not to miss any things of great importance. I struggled to see beyond the crowd and concentrate on its bowels, beyond the faces and hearts of each individual, to understand each one. I sensed that Jesus was doing this and expected me to join Him. So I did.

God noticed my anguish and was pleased to see me dig deeper to personalize my experience. Pleased that I quickly realized the importance of noticing the most significant aspects of the crowds, God said, "Don't worry, Bill, you are doing great. I can sense your mind patiently looking past the unimportant things and piercing in on the most important. Do not worry about anything. It can only slow you down and challenge your godly instincts."

After God's pep talk, I could tell an immediate and more intelligent skill set was kicking in. I could now evaluate every person in these masses with qualities I never remember having. I now had circumspection, discernment, discrimination, and an instinctiveness that, seconds ago, I barely knew the meaning of.

Many in the crowd were genuine supporters who had been following Jesus for quite a while and truly loved Him. They would become the very first Christians, who, like Jesus, would be persecuted and possibly killed for their faith. Most of them, however, seemed to have no idea of what lay ahead. They could not see a need for a Messiah to suffer and die. They could not fathom the idea that the kingdom Jesus promised would be eternal and heavenly rather than temporal and earthly. They looked to a destiny of being saved from the oppression of Roman rule, not from the oppression of their sins. Since Jesus knew what was coming, it most likely made Him sad for them. I was!

It was easy for me to pick out His enemies in the crowd. There was no love in their eyes as Jesus passed. Instead, there was pure hatred. It seemed I could almost feel the heat of this loathing. And I could tell much of what they were thinking. "Why is He riding that colt rather than a beautiful and majestic white horse, more suitable for a king?"

It was also apparent that many more in the crowd were simply curiosity seekers who show up at parades, hoping to catch a glimpse of the current celebrity. As they nonchalantly waved their palms, they nudged their neighbor to ask the identity of this person on a colt. I could even read some of their lips as one would say to another, "Who is this man anyway?" And those in the crowd would often respond with "He is a prophet from Nazareth in Galilee, a man called Jesus." I could sense their disappointment upon hearing this, as they often responded, "Who?" and then walked away.

I observed activities in the crowd that were quite ominous. I recognized some religious leaders who had been at the banquet for Lazarus. Once again, they were up to no good. They walked along with the flow of the crowd but seemed to stay at a safe distance. There was no mistaking their presence in the crowd, standing there in their fine robes, long hanging tassels, extra prayer boxes, and haughty posture. They looked around at the crowd as if hoping others would notice them. They enjoyed the reactions and attention from many in the crowd who recognized them and gave them exactly what they wanted—respect, high esteem, awe, admiration, and even reverence.

Some from the crowd looked like they were reporting to the Pharisees. These suspicious groups would huddle together, appearing to be in serious discussion. Every so often, they would look at Jesus, and there would be nothing but contempt and hatred in their eyes. It was a look of pure evil—and bone-chilling to me. I hoped never to see them again, but unfortunately, I knew better than that. Yet Jesus showed no emotion, as if He had never noticed them. But of course, I knew He had, since I had.

One from each group would run ahead to several men who I assumed were Pharisees by their formality, demeanor, and cockiness. They now attempted to be less conspicuous by backing into darkened doorways, but they still stuck out to me. Runners would periodically report everything they had learned and then run ahead to a later section in the crowd.

The ones reporting to the Pharisees may have been Pharisees, but it was unclear since they were dressed more like everyone else. They might have thought that Jesus would not recognize them for who they were or their agenda. Several times, they approached Jesus with questions. One of their questions concerned the crowd's verbal proclamations about Jesus. They yelled loudly at Jesus, demanding that He rebuke the crowds for their blasphemy when proclaiming Him to be God. Jesus responded that if these people remained silent, the stones would cry out. By the look on their faces, I could tell that they had no idea what this meant. Nor did I … to be honest.

Jesus's response sure got rid of them as they scurried back to the crowd's edge to give another update to the Pharisee leaders. I could tell from how they'd react to Jesus's answers that they knew they had been rebuked, but they seemed confused about exactly how He had done it. Of course, this confusion further angered them, and they finally left the parade—probably to conspire further. I would have sensed a feeling of glee over the victory, but I could not because Jesus did not emote any such prideful and vindictive emotion.

Another group stood out as we were about to enter the city. Numerous Roman soldiers acted as if they had no interest in the procession other than ensuring it was orderly and peaceful. They seemed to be completely bored. The only emotion they ever showed was irritation—with some of the Pharisees coming up to them. The Pharisees were trying to get the soldiers to disperse the crowd while angrily pointing at Jesus. The soldiers motioned them to move along, failing to show them the respect they felt they deserved.

I would remember some of these soldiers' faces several days later when they would be more interested in Jesus and treat Him much more to the Pharisees' liking.

Just as we entered Jerusalem, I felt Jesus look away from the crowd and toward the city before us. Jesus was quite intent on the temple that stood in the distance. And for the second time in less than a week, Jesus wept, and once again, I was momentarily confused as to the reason. To most, it would have been considered a triumphant entry into the city. Were these possibly tears of joy? Of course not! More than likely, it was the rejection we saw in the eyes of so many in the crowd of His foretelling of the ominous nature of the upcoming week. He may have blamed the city for having killed the prophets and stoned God's messengers. Maybe He knew (of course He knew—since He was God) what would eventually become of this beautiful city, temple, and chosen race of people. Or it may have been a combination of all these things!

I was sad, and I cried along with Jesus for the first time.

So far on this trip, God the Father had been stoic, patient, and restrained. He had shown few emotions that I could detect. But this was different. I sensed that God the Father was experiencing the same emotions as Jesus, His Son.

I had many questions but knew this was no time to bring them up to God. I'd have to wait until later—possibly much later.

CHAPTER SIX

CHAOS IN THE TEMPLE

T he procession to Jerusalem from the Mount of Olives was complete. The crowds wondered where Jesus would go next, but it was clear in His mind. He was going to the temple to observe if the behavior of the worshippers and leaders had once again deteriorated into blasphemy, as it had at the previous Passover celebration.

We stood there for a moment at the entrance to the city. We could see the magnificent temple rising above the rooftops of the houses and businesses in between. It was amazingly beautiful. Herod the Great had outdone himself in its restoration and renovations. Herod had spared no cost.

Although it was not expensive for the Jews in monetary terms, it was an extremely steep price to pay in terms of their integrity. Herod had not created a masterpiece out of the goodness of his heart or any allegiance to God. It was no more than a political donation, insurance payment, and bribe to the Jewish leaders in exchange for their support. It assured Herod that the Jewish leaders would be content with the status quo as a conquered and submissive people. They, in return, would allow nothing to occur among the people that might disturb the fragile political climate. Although it had been a costly project for Herod to finance, it was still a low price to pay to assure the region's stability.

After passing through the Golden Gate and entering the city, Jesus went directly toward the temple. We walked slowly through the streets and looked around in amazement. Our mood became quite somber as we started moving in the general direction of the temple. I assumed the temple would be our initial destination, since Jesus loved the time He had spent there—worshipping God, ministering to the spiritually starved people, and discussing issues with the religious leaders. As we got closer and closer to the temple, Jesus quickened His pace and narrowed His focus. There was now only one thing we could see—the temple. We looked neither to the left nor the right. We were oblivious to the crowds and the chaos in the streets. Jesus's mood changed from somber to something much stronger. It was anger. Not hatred. Simply anger—controlled anger, intense anger.

But why?

As we reached the temple, it became apparent why Jesus was so livid. It was not so much what we saw when we looked at the thousands of people milling around outside the temple. It was what we did not see. What was not happening? There were no merchants. There were no money changers. And if they were not outside the temple, they most assuredly must be on the inside, once again polluting this holy place.

Jesus reminded us of the last time He visited the temple. It was also during Passover week. Then, just as now, He had found money changers, merchants, and tax collectors inside the temple, making a mockery of the intended temple worship by conducting their fraudulent commercial enterprises. At that time, Jesus had chased all of them out into the streets, scattering their money and turning over their tables. Jesus warned us at the time that they would surely return. He was right.

I held my breath. What was about to happen? How would Jesus react?

As we entered the temple, we went directly to the court of the Gentiles, overflowing with pilgrims, merchants, tax collectors, and money changers, all pressing up against each other, barely able to move. As Jesus surveyed the chaos, looking slowly around the court, we saw the merchants and money changers pretending not to notice Jesus, but they were keeping a close eye on Him. They continued to conduct business but never let Jesus out of sight. Nor did Jesus take His eyes from them.

I could hear the many voices of those taking advantage of these pilgrims who had come so far. There were merchants loudly reminding the Gentiles that they could purchase inferior sacrificial animals at prices much higher than they were worth. Money changers then directed them to booths where they could exchange their home country's currency for temple currency at usurious rates. And corrupt tax collectors were herding pilgrims to where the exorbitant temple tax could be paid. These "services" came at a very steep price for the pilgrims. After all, everyone but the pilgrims would get their "fair" share of profits from these unfair practices.

To make matters even worse, the area used for these blasphemous activities was also designated for worship. This left no room to worship, kneel, or prostrate oneself before the Lord. There was no peace, no quiet, no place of solitude in this place belonging to God.

The countenance of the pilgrims was one of disgust and contempt. They hated being cheated. They hated being controlled. They hated being manipulated. They hated the overt hypocrisy of these so-called religious leaders.

I sensed Jesus's growing disgust, anger, and sadness, but it was accompanied by intense love. He remained calm. Yes, there would be punishment for these obscene activities, and the punishment would be harsh. But I sensed absolutely no hatred within Jesus—only love. He had come for those He was most angered by, those who hated Him the most, and those who would reject Him, betray Him, and ignore Him. I had trouble understanding that. I knew that Jesus was not necessarily a consistent God, but how could He still have this constant love and compassion for those who wanted so little of Him or had nothing to do with Him?

People like me!

I turned to the Father and asked, "How can You and Jesus exert only love but not hate? I could not do that unless I had to, which I am now doing, but only because Jesus is directing my emotions to match His own."

The Father sweetly responded, "Remember, in all ways, be like Jesus." Of course I knew He was right, but did He answer my question?

Then the heavy weight of conviction fell on me. I was no better than the money changers, the merchants, the tax collectors, and the Pharisees. No better than anyone else. I was just as much the hypocrite as those I had so proudly judged for their treatment of Jesus. I had not treated Jesus any better than they had. I was no less a sinner than these despicable individuals.

I pleaded with God to help me understand. "How can Jesus demonstrate the extent of His love? The love He has for me and them and all of us? I have so much trouble expanding my mind and heart to comprehend Your love's vastness."

But then the sweet feeling that I shared with Jesus was overpowering the effort of Satan to keep me from understanding. For the first time, I gained insight into how it feels to love your enemy and realized that without Jesus within me, and now me within Jesus, it would not, it could not, be possible. I still had a great deal of trouble fully understanding it, but I was intensely appreciating being able to experience it firsthand.

I hoped I would never forget this glorious moment with Jesus, always feel the same intense appreciation when I returned to my everyday life, and embrace it for my remaining time on earth. I then asked God the Father, "Will I be able to carry these intentions back to my normal life?"

He responded very sweetly, saying, "Of course you can. Let's talk more when we get home. Give me a call, and we'll talk."

"You're on," I said. "And thanks. Sorry, I can't think of a better way to express my feelings now."

Just when it appeared that Jesus might take no aggressive and overt action, He once again drove everyone from the temple and out into the streets. Quoting the prophets Isaiah and Jeremiah, Jesus shouted, "The Scriptures declare, 'My temple will be called a place of prayer,' but you have turned it into a den of thieves." The offending parties immediately scattered, chaotically trying to secure as much of their property as possible before they had to find a forced exit to the street.

Although there was unbelievable excitement within the temple, I knew Jesus felt no sense of exhilaration. There was nothing to celebrate. Instead, Jesus grieved for Jerusalem, His temple, and the deceivers and those they deceived. He grieved for those He loved so much who had disappointed Him so much. I also grieved with Him. It was my honor to do so.

CHAPTER SEVEN

LEADING UP TO THE PASSOVER

After the merchants and money changers scurried from the temple and into the streets, we spent that day and the few that followed inside the temple, ensuring the den of thieves could not return. They would have to conduct their thievery somewhere else. The religious and political leaders, however, did not withdraw. They were always there asking Jesus questions, lurking in the shadows, and listening while we met with the crowds who came to the temple. Although they hoped to find some way to entrap Jesus into saying something incriminating that could be used against Him, they were never able to do so. Most of their time in the temple was spent being embarrassed or confused. They were never a match for Jesus.

It was interesting to behold, watching the religious leaders come and go when they were sure they had finally worked out the perfect trap for Jesus. Especially intriguing was the "tag team" approach of the Pharisees and Sadducees, who one might have thought were working together if it were not for their apparent dislike for each other. One or more of the Pharisees (sometimes pretending to be genuinely interested in Jesus's message) would approach Jesus with what they thought would produce an answer from Jesus that would be self-incriminating. They were such prideful gluttons for punishment.

Jesus, however, could always answer in a way that completely confused them, leaving the Pharisees to retreat like dogs with their tails between their legs. With every answer a perfect response, the exchanges between Jesus and the Jewish leaders hardly seemed a fair match.

Then the Sadducees would come forward with their attempt to discredit Jesus, thinking they could do better than the Pharisees had done. Yet, they would soon become the ones being discredited, limping off to consider some new tactic.

It was ingenious how Jesus responded to their questions and accusations, almost without thinking. It was as if He knew what it would be before they even asked a question. It was also as if His responses had been planned and carefully rehearsed. But of course, there was a reason for this. After all, since Jesus is truly God and man, He must have known their questions and His answers in advance.

Jesus used a confounding variety of approaches when dealing with religious leaders. Sometimes, He would answer a question with another question that the religious leaders did not feel comfortable answering. For example, He used this approach when they demanded to know by what authority He had driven the merchants out of the temple. Jesus told them He would answer their question, but only if they'd first tell Him where John the Baptist had gotten his baptism authority. Realizing that any answer they gave would be a lose-lose for them, they decided to respond with "We do not know." The look on their faces was a priceless combination of defeat and embarrassment. Many in the crowd reacted with amazement at what appeared to be their ignorance, with some bystanders being moved to mocking laughter. Very few people had ever been willing or able to confront the religious leaders previously, and none had ever outwitted them so quickly.

I felt like shouting, "Attaboy, Jesus," but I quickly realized how inappropriate it would be. Jesus would never act that way.

Sometimes, Jesus would respond with a parable, the meaning of which was not immediately apparent to His antagonists. When they realized its meaning, it was too late to avoid being confounded and humiliated. One of the parables Jesus told them concerned an evil farmer who murdered anyone the property owner sent (including the owner's son) to collect the owner's share of the crop. When asked what they would do, the religious leaders replied that the evil farmer must be put to a horrible death and that the property should be given to others who were deserving of receiving it.

Little did the religious leaders realize, until after they had answered, that they were the subject of the parable. They were the evil farmer; the land was the kingdom of heaven, and they would be the ones to lose their place in the kingdom. Once again, they were shamed in front of a large audience, and their anger, resentment, and plotting intensified.

Other times, Jesus would harshly and directly verbally attack the Jewish leaders for their lack of integrity, compassion, and knowledge. He compared them to the son who made a promise to his father but was disobedient in his failure to fulfill his responsibility. They were also compared to wedding guests who ignored the invitations to the wedding feast and shamefully treated the messengers the master sent. But amazingly, no matter how pointed and critical Jesus was of the religious leaders, there was never a hint of anger, contempt, pride, or animosity in His voice. Jesus never acted smug or vindictive, which I felt He had every right to be. But that was how Jesus always was, hoping people would be convicted of their sins and turn back to God. It brought Him no joy to triumph over those who repeatedly rejected Him.

A thought came to mind. *I could never respond this way to people who hate me and will later have me put to death. I can't understand how Jesus is so patient with these people.*

You could tell by the look in their eyes and the tone of their voices how intense their loathing was. Jesus knew that they would never give up their zeal to have Him killed.

Jesus also knew that they would become even more ruthless. With no guilt and complete disregard for the same laws they unmercifully enforced against others, they would next resort to lies and illegal activities. Whatever it would take—they would not give up. Their only genuine concern was that it must be accomplished in a way that would not instigate an uprising among Jesus's supporters and force a violent response from the Romans!

Amazingly, Jesus always treated them with both love and sadness in His heart. The same love caused Him to come to earth in the first place. And it was the same sadness He had in knowing where they would spend eternity for their choices.

Eventually, the leaders stopped coming forward to challenge Jesus, though many stayed within a close distance to hear what Jesus was saying to the pilgrims. Jesus spent most of His time with the crowds that gathered to listen to Him. He repeatedly warned the people not to trust the religious leaders, referring to them as ignorant of Scripture, hypocrites, unjust, merciless, faithless, blind guides, unclean, murderers, snakes, sons of vipers, and cheaters. Even worse, since they were teachers, they had significant responsibilities and would be severely punished.

The crowd was mesmerized, listening to Him with great interest. They seemed to hang on every word. But very few seemed to understand who He was, why He had come, and why He had to die if He was indeed the Messiah. A few people came to believe it, but many were afraid to admit it to anyone else.

Jesus explained to the listeners that many people could not believe, fulfilling Isaiah's prophecy that God had blinded their eyes and hardened their hearts so they could not see or understand. That confused me.

Why would God make sure that people could not believe in Him? I wanted to ask the Father to explain why this was true. But I was afraid He would consider my question a challenge rather than a simple curiosity, so I decided not to bother Him. Of course, I also knew that God knew what I was thinking. I did not have to speak to be heard by Him. So I decided to try to figure it out independently. I hoped that God would respect me for making the effort.

Several possibilities came to mind as I sought to find answers. Was this to fulfill the prophecy? Was it because their understanding was incomplete at best and would require Jesus's death and resurrection for them to have a more complete picture? Were they blinded because of their unwillingness to consider the Messiah as anything but a military leader? Was Jesus planting the seeds and allowing the disciples to experience the joy of harvesting the crop when the same people were among the thousands who would accept Him after His resurrection?

I had to accept the possibility that I might never know. At least not by the time I returned to my everyday life. It would be another of the many things I would consider later.

After spending an exhausting day with the religious leaders and Passover pilgrims each night, we would return to the Mount of Olives, near the city, where we could see the temple below. At this time and on the trips to and from the city, Jesus taught the disciples what they needed to know after He was gone. One of the things Jesus talked to us about was the destiny of the temple and its ultimate destruction. Despite what might be coming, Jesus warned us not to despair. I could still tell by the looks on their faces that this news scared the disciples, even though they were not sure what to make of it.

Jesus taught about His return in a cloud and the need to be vigilant. Jesus spoke about the kingdom of God using a variety of parables. Each parable emphasized the need to be alert to when Jesus would return. When His disciples pressed Jesus for a definite time for His return, Jesus told them that only the Father in heaven knows the time. Not even the angels in heaven nor the Son Himself knows. I found it fascinating that although Jesus is fully God, He does not know everything that will happen. Only the Father does.

The last subject Jesus taught during our quiet times with Him involved the final judgment. Although there was no indication when precisely this would occur, I sensed that the disciples thought it would be much sooner rather than later. I doubt they felt that two thousand years later, we would still be wondering the same thing.

I then reflected on how I had a much better idea of when the return of Jesus would come than the people who were now talking and walking with Jesus. Although none of us know, my generation has a good idea since Israel's return to its original home occurred in 1948, and the book of

Revelation prophesied Jesus would return during the generation of Jewish people who have returned.

What a week this has already been for me. But it is nothing like what we will face when Passover begins.

CHAPTER EIGHT

THE LAST SUPPER

This week became unbelievably hectic as we approached the Passover. The disciples knew that the religious leaders were planning something everywhere they went, although they had no idea where or when it would occur. They sensed our need to be near or part of large crowds just in case the religious leaders tried something in public. Jesus, however, assured the disciples that it didn't matter how large the crowds were or where we met, that whatever was going to happen would be precisely when, where, and how God wanted it to happen. We took no special precautions each night while staying at the Mount of Olives.

Surely, the religious leaders knew where we were. They knew we were highly vulnerable. But Jesus assured us not to worry. He'd say, "All in God's time." That was it! And it always calmed all but one of us.

Judas was always jittery and often acted strangely. It was as though he had lost his focus. He used to hang on every word that Jesus spoke, just like the rest of us. Yes, he was always much more concerned with the financial affairs of the ministry than anyone else. And yes, he always seemed to be looking in from outside the group. But this week, he appeared to have lost most of any passion he may have had. In addition, Judas showed great impatience with Jesus, becoming quite emphatic that Jesus clarified His intentions to gather greater support from the people. "Before it is too late," he would say.

Judas was often away from the group as we spent time in the temple. He would wander off without explaining. Each night at the Mount of

Olives, he seemed distracted, deep in thought, and less interested in what Jesus taught. He was going through some intense emotional struggles, but he was unwilling to share them with the rest of us. Jesus treated him with respect and love, never hinting at what He knew would be Judas's role in His death.

Jesus finally clarified where we would celebrate the Passover dinner, something the disciples had been wondering about. Two days before Passover, Jesus instructed Peter and John to go to a house nearby, which a strong supporter of Jesus owned. Jesus assured them that the house owner would make a large upstairs room available to them—one already set up for the dinner. Once they found the house, they were to prepare dinner according to the Passover requirements.

Doing what Jesus asked, Peter and John soon returned, reporting that the room had been found just as Jesus had predicted and that the dinner had been prepared. It was time for the Passover dinner, an evening far from what everyone expected.

When we arrived at the Upper Room, Peter and John began bickering as they often did. Previously, they had asked Jesus to allow them to sit next to Him in heaven, for which they were greatly chastised. This time, their argument was over where they would sit. Once again, they both wanted to be in a place of honor next to Jesus, but of the two, only John was allowed to do so. He would sit at Jesus's right hand. Since it was customary for the group treasurer to sit next to the master, Judas sat immediately to the left of Jesus, leaving Peter to scramble for a lesser position at the table. The best he could do was to find a seat immediately across from Jesus. Although he was nearly as close to Jesus as John, Peter lacked the prestige he longed for.

Jesus was not surprised by their behavior, but it saddened Him—at such a critical moment—to endure such pettiness from His closest friends. I felt His sadness more than ever.

However, it was not just Peter and John who were disagreeable. Most of the other disciples were arguing with each other over who was the most important. I suppose it was natural for them to wonder what each of their roles would be in heaven because of the extensive time Jesus had spent this past week discussing the kingdom of God. But their ill temper sprang from much more than simple curiosity. They were also arguing about who would be the most important in the kingdom: what would be their "pecking order"?

If I had been Jesus, I would have scolded them harshly, but it was obvious that Jesus now had more important and pressing thoughts and concerns on His mind. Even though He had taught the disciples well, they still had a minimal understanding of what much of His teaching meant. Indeed, understanding and maturity would come, but there was very little time before they would be completely on their own.

The disciples had expected the Passover dinner to be the same as they had experienced every other year of their lives and the last two Passovers spent with Jesus. But Jesus surprised them with numerous revisions of the traditional observance.

He shocked them with new revelations about His impending betrayal and death. He compared the Passover lamb to Himself and said that the bread and wine we ate were His body and blood. He made it quite clear that He was about to die, that His body was about to be torn apart and His blood shed in the process. Even though Jesus had been giving us many warnings of His impending death, it was still hard to accept that it was about to happen.

Following dinner, Jesus filled a large bowl with water, went to each of the disciples—and knelt in front of them. He began to wash their feet and dry them with a towel. I could tell by the shocked look on their faces that each disciple felt a multitude of emotions. I could sense confusion and embarrassment. Although they could not speak, their eyes seemed to scream: "What is He doing? This is all wrong! Shouldn't servants be doing this? Should we be doing it? Who will wash His feet?"

As Jesus humbly worked around the table, I observed Peter getting increasingly anxious as Jesus approached Him. He looked perplexed, as if he was unable—or maybe unwilling—to accept Jesus in a servant's role.

Perhaps Peter felt it was simply beneath Jesus for Him to wash his and the other disciples' feet. Maybe Peter could not imagine himself carrying out a similar role as a servant to others. Certainly, he would be honored to wash the feet of Jesus, but he'd prefer not to think about doing it for the other disciples, much less strangers. When Jesus finally reached him, Peter was unwilling to participate. He later grudgingly consented, but only after Jesus clarified that being one of His disciples required accepting a servant's role.

With apparent anguish and sadness, Jesus declared, "The truth is, one of you will betray Me." It had to be one of the disciples—and, therefore, one of Jesus's closest friends. No one else was in the room. Of course, I knew who it was, whom others may have suspected, but all the rest acted as if they had no idea.

As Jesus looked around the table, I could see the shock on everyone's face—with one significant exception. Judas looked down. After a moment of stunned and distressed silence, each disciple asked Jesus the same question—"I am not the one, am I?" as if hoping that Jesus would assure the one asking the question that He did not have him in mind. Jesus said nothing to allay their fears, however.

When Judas asked Jesus about who was betraying Him, saying, "Surely it is not I, Rabbi?" Jesus said to him, "You have said it yourself." No one understood exactly what Jesus meant, so they turned to each other, telling whoever would listen that it was surely not him. They could not be the one Jesus was referring to! It was hard to tell if the disciples were trying to convince the others that they could not be traitors or trying to convince themselves.

As they spoke to each other, it was evident that Judas showed no sincerity when he expressed his "Surely I am not the one" to several other disciples. I assumed that the disciples were so concerned about proving their innocence that they were oblivious to the evident guilt and insincerity of another.

Sitting across from Jesus, Peter made numerous attempts to attract John's attention, nodding in Jesus's direction and trying to persuade John to ask Jesus, "Who is it?" Finally, John reluctantly leaned over to Jesus, quietly asking, "Lord, who is it?"

Jesus, clearly having heard him, responded, "It is the one to whom I give the bread dipped in the sauce."

Jesus then turned to Judas. I noticed Judas's deep and evil demeanor as Jesus looked deeply into his eyes. Judas did not look confused or hurt like the other disciples. Instead, he bore an intense look of determination and decisiveness. He appeared impatient, as if waiting for something to happen. It seemed he was struggling to leave—but somehow could not. He also appeared to be in a trance, as if he were under the control of something quite evil.

In another moment, Jesus offered Judas the cup and said, "What you are doing, do it quickly." Judas immediately got up and left the room. It was as if Jesus had just permitted Judas to go, and only then could he do so. Judas acted like a marionette with two puppeteers—one evil and one perfectly good.

As Judas left the room, I noticed the money bag that always hung from his belt. It was now quite full, making a loud and unexpected jingling noise. Judas had already collected his blood money. There would be no going back for him now!

No one tried to stop Judas. Perhaps they had not heard Jesus speak to him. Or they may not have known the significance of what Jesus said to him. It certainly looked as though Jesus might have sent him on an errand related to the meal.

But John had heard. He knew where Judas was going. Didn't he? Why hadn't John said something or done something? Surely he knew what it meant. He must have heard Jesus's answer concerning who would betray Him. Why did he do nothing to stop Judas? Or did he somehow know that if he had tried to stop Judas, Jesus would not have let him?

Jesus turned to the remaining disciples and told them that they, too, would betray Him when He needed them the most—through their desertion, inattention, and denials. Peter immediately protested, assuring Jesus that he would die for Jesus. That he would never betray Him. In a knowing and sympathetic manner, Jesus told Peter that he would deny Him three times before the rooster crowed the following morning. Despite Peter's protests, he no longer seemed as confident as he had been. After all, Jesus had never been wrong before.

Little did Peter know how accurate Jesus was, how soon it would happen, and how devastated he would be after his betrayal of his Lord.

Jesus was ready to leave, so we immediately left the room and returned to the Mount of Olives. The disciples went with confusion in their minds, pain in their hearts, and fear in their guts. I felt a potpourri of emotions coming from Jesus. There was determination and focus. There was sadness. And yes, I even sensed some fear. I said to myself, *Can even Jesus be afraid?*

I wondered if God had heard me. Had I been sacrilegious? I know that Jesus was now a human in all ways except sin. But is fear even a sin? God said nothing. What did that mean? I hoped I had not disappointed God.

CHAPTER NINE

THE LAST WALK TO THE GARDEN

W hen it finally came time to leave the Upper Room, we started our walk to the garden of Gethsemane on the Mount of Olives. We had spent the last few nights there. One difference was that Judas was not with us. Another was that we walked in complete and stunned silence. The disciples seemed overwhelmed as they reflected on what they had heard and seen in the previous hours and days. I could see a variety of emotions on their faces. Most of them appeared confused, probably trying to piece together the significance of everything that had just taken place. Many looked fearful, unclear about their immediate and distant futures.

But they were still where they needed to be, following Jesus wherever He took them. They had remained loyal to Jesus almost to the very end. But not quite! There was still a lot to come.

During the week, I could tell the disciples were becoming increasingly nervous each night as we returned to the same place to pray, talk, and sleep. It would not be hard for our enemies to figure out where we went each night. In addition, rumors were passing around that religious leaders were looking for a private opportunity to have Jesus arrested and ultimately killed. And now, after observing Judas's erratic behavior at dinner, what Jesus accused him of, and his abrupt exit from the room, there was little doubt that Judas was a traitor and wanted his promised payoff sooner rather than later. He would probably go to the religious leaders to encourage them to act before Jesus could slip away into His massive cult of believers.

Conditions were right for the religious leaders to feel comfortable in taking action. The garden provided a more private place to arrest Jesus. There would be no crowd to object or respond to. It was close by and quickly accessible. We would undoubtedly be outnumbered. But as always, Jesus seemed to be at complete peace as He assured us that returning to the same place was necessary. So they followed, and no one offered any opposition.

Returning to the exact location, I imagined the disciples nervously thinking about whether it was safe to return one last time. And, yet they said nothing. They thought they knew what they had signed up for with Jesus. But even at the late date, did they? Were they ready for what was coming?

Just before we entered the garden, Jesus broke the silence, once again warning the disciples that they would soon fall away from Him, be scattered like sheep, and deny Him. He had issued a similar prophetic warning a short time earlier in the Upper Room, where Peter had passionately rejected the possibility—the actuality—of Jesus's predictions coming true.

This time, all the disciples were confused by what Jesus was saying. They assured Jesus they would never be disloyal; they would go to their death for Him—if needed.

As I observed the disciples' reactions, I was baffled. Jesus was telling them in no uncertain terms what would occur. Not what might occur! Not what could occur or would occur if they were not careful. Scripture prophesied what would occur, and Jesus repeatedly said the scriptures about Him must be fulfilled.

And yet the disciples dismissed what Jesus told them. They did not fall on their knees at the prospect of betraying Him, ask for His forgiveness, plead with Him to change their fate, or even resolve and make plans to avoid that fate. They pridefully rejected the possibility of these prophecies ever occurring. They seemed confident that Jesus was wrong! Yes, wrong! It sounded to me like blasphemy!

I then realized that if indeed—or when indeed—they did scatter, fall, deny, and betray Jesus, it would be more a result of their hardheaded pride rather than their lack of courage, intent, or loyalty. Especially Peter! When

Jesus told him that he would deny his Lord three times before the cock crowed the next morning, Peter again emotionally denied it adamantly, insisting that, whereas the other disciples might fall away from Jesus, the prophecy could not apply to him. He would stand strong—even if he were the only one to do so!

I felt Jesus subtly shaking His head in frustration—or was it sadness? I sensed that Jesus was thinking silently, *Never say I didn't warn you, Peter.*

That night in the garden, there would be no more teaching, discussion, or learning about the future. But there would be prayer. Things were about to come to a head. Jesus took Peter, James, and John—and me—away from the others so that we would not be interrupted if Judas and the accompanying soldiers came early. He asked them to be watchful as He went a short distance away to pray, asking that they would not enter into temptation. He was filled with distress and anguish as He lamented, "My soul is crushed with grief to the point of death."

As this pain came upon Jesus, I knew I would also be suffering along with Him. It was quite an intimidating thought! I had no idea what to expect or how bad it would be. God had told me I would share Jesus's suffering pain but not to the same extent. I tried to remain strong as it began, since I had no idea how extreme it would get. I told God, "Please help me get through this so I can finally appreciate—at least a little bit—what Jesus is going through."

As our pain increased, I assumed that Jesus wanted the disciples to watch for anyone approaching the garden from the city. It should be easy for them since the night was pitch black. And a large group would need to carry many torches to find their way.

I wondered why Jesus asked them to report to Him. Did He not already know when they would be arriving? Was He testing them? Or did He want them to remember later how they had failed when He needed their help the most … and that their prayers would have diminished His pain?

Had He planned an escape? Of course not! He would never do that. I was embarrassed even thinking it—for I knew—and of course, He knew what Scripture clearly said. I was hoping that somehow there would be a different outcome, but I knew there could not be.

I wondered about Jesus's specific request of Peter, James, and John—that they pray to resist temptation. I assumed the request related to the temptations they would soon face to deny Him, betray Him, or desert Him. But He had already told them that they would do these things, not just that they would be tempted to do them. Could their prayer at this time have helped them resist their temptations, even though the prophecies had to come true? Or would the present warnings be something for the disciples to reflect on, reminding them that Jesus had given them one last chance to avoid doing what they would later do?

While the disciples slept, Jesus and I began to experience something horrific, causing excruciating mental pain and suffering as if we were being tortured. We were distressed, grieving, troubled, distraught, anxious, and anguished—and yet with no physical explanation of who was torturing us. And I knew that as bad as it was for me, it had to be indescribable for Jesus. I asked God to give both of us the strength to continue, and there was His assurance that, indeed, He would.

But then, Satan had an impact on me that was a total surprise. I had assumed that my time with Jesus would protect me from Satan's access to me. But evidently, He could still pierce my mind and thereby tempt me. I know Jesus was still tempted, so why shouldn't I be also? But I was at my weakest point. I was experiencing more in the garden than I imag-ined—and so was Jesus. And yet I felt only a fraction of what Jesus was experiencing.

So how could I complain? But I did! I never realized how much the emotional or physical toll would be. I never expected it to be this terrible. I knew it was still very little compared to what Jesus was enduring, even though Satan kept telling me that I was the only one suffering and that Jesus always allowed others to suffer for Him. Satan so hoped I would believe him or criticize Jesus for this. But I would not! I did not! I finally said, "Thank You, Lord."

But I was still tempted to yell to God, "Stop! Please stop! Please stop! I can't take any more of this!" I even thought about what Satan had told just me and, for an instant, considered whether it could be true. But then God told me: "Bill, I know this is difficult for you, but imagine how it is for Jesus. It's time you remember all I've taught you—all you know that is true in My Bible, one of My many gifts to you. And everything you know is true concerning Satan. He is evil! And he always lies! Do not listen to him—not tonight, not ever. Do not even consider anything you may think might have come straight from his lips. Get back to praying! It will soothe your pain and comfort Jesus greatly."

Jesus's sweat soaked His clothes, dropped onto the ground at His knees, and ran down a slight hill to where Peter, James, and John were fast asleep. The intensity of what we were experiencing was so forceful that Jesus soon became completely dehydrated. He had no water left to deplete through His sweat glands. His body was forced to drain the only liquids He had remaining—His blood. So as He continued to pray in agony, Jesus's blood forced its way through His skin, eventually reaching the stream that was still moving down the hill.

As Jesus prayed in great anguish to be relieved of the sufferings we were experiencing, I could tell He knew all too well that there was no relief in sight, at least not for a while. It seemed to me that Jesus was fearful—I certainly felt it—of what was about to occur. But thankfully, this emotion lasted only for an instant. Any fear He might have had quickly turned to trust as He told His Father that He would follow Him no matter where it took Him. He also looked to the disciples for support through their prayers, but they had already emotionally deserted Him by falling asleep thrice. We had to suffer through this agonizing hour by ourselves. I was unable to do anything but suffer with Him and pray. And I wondered how much less our suffering might have been if the disciples had not fallen asleep each time instead of praying with Him.

When it seemed like the ordeal would be too great for us, Our Father sent an angel to provide us the strength we needed. It was as if the angel had come to wrap Jesus and me within God's cloak of protection, allowing us to stand firm inside the armor of God. We were both clothed with the belt of truth, the shoes of peace, the breastplate of righteousness, the helmet of salvation, and the shield of faith. And His sword of faith would pierce the temptations that Satan would bring in a constant barrage. Eventually, peace would prevail.

No single disciple stayed awake as Jesus struggled with the burden He assumed. Not one noticed the contortions on His face when He returned three times to find them asleep. When He wakened them, not one noticed His bloodstained clothes. Not one noticed the winding line of torches that crept along the road to the garden despite their being instructed to keep watch.

Jesus and I knew of the arrival of the large group close to entering the garden. He pointed out that the one who would betray Him was at hand. With Peter, James, and John, we rejoined the rest of the disciples. There, we met with the first of many who wanted Jesus dead.

The first thing I looked for was the religious leaders. They would undoubtedly be here to let Jesus know they had won, that Jesus would soon die a terrible death, and that His followers would scatter in every direction. But I could not see a single religious leader in the crowd. Were they afraid they would meet armed opposition from Jesus's followers? Were they unwilling to get their hands dirty with any violence that took place? Granted, Jesus's followers had never been violent before, but who knew what could happen now?

The religious leaders had stayed back and sent a band of soldiers who I assumed would be Romans. But they were not Romans. Instead, the band seemed to be a cohort of officers from the temple under the authority of the chief priests and Pharisees.

In front of them all stood Judas—who led them straight to Jesus. Before they spoke, Jesus asked who they were looking for, to which they responded, "Jesus the Nazarene!" When Jesus answered, "I am He," it was as if Jesus's voice was that of an earthquake, as the ground suddenly began shaking. All the uninvited guests fell to the ground. Holding to each other, they struggled to rise, once again having to answer Jesus's simple question about who they came for. This time, however, the answer prompted them to turn to Judas as if they needed him to verify that the one who answered was indeed Jesus, the one they had come for.

They certainly could not return to the city with the wrong man. So they must have been concerned that Jesus might escape by substituting someone else for Himself to avoid arrest. Judas came forward as if on cue, drew close to Jesus, and looked like he was about to kiss Jesus. Without a hint of sarcasm, contempt, or anger, Jesus called Judas "friend," told him to do what he came to do, and allowed the Judas kiss to take place.

Knowing that Jesus was about to be arrested, the disciples looked to Jesus for permission to use their swords in defense, and Peter, not waiting for an answer, impulsively cut off the ear of the high priest's slave. However, before any fight ensued, Jesus calmly prevented the disciples from further action, reminding them that He could have had twelve legions of angels come to His defense if He wanted. Jesus healed the slave's ear, told the crowd that his arrest must take place to fulfill Scripture, and allowed them to arrest Him. At once, the disciples, who had just a moment before offered to fight to the death—fled into the night—one and all! Or more specifically, everyone but me!

Even though I went wherever Jesus did, I felt quite nervous for the first time. None of my newest friends stayed. I felt quite lonely. The Bible has no discussion of the treatment during the walk back to Jerusalem.

As we were being dragged out of the garden in chains, Jesus looked back, and we caught a glimpse of Peter and James, who were now following at a safe distance. John was also spotted, barely escaping his potential captors, who were left holding nothing but a linen sheet. None of the other disciples were visible—they must have left earlier.

I had to wonder what Peter was thinking. Did he pridefully feel vindicated that he had shown courage in taking the action he did in cutting off the ear of the slave? Did he feel ashamed that he had fled with the others to avoid his arrest? Was he now following the procession to prove that Jesus was wrong about the denials He had predicted? Or was he drawn to follow, thinking he might still be able to rescue Jesus from the fate that Peter most likely still could not understand? Might Peter be able to reverse the series of events that had begun to spin out of control?

I then thanked God for helping me survive all that we had just experienced, and I began to think ahead to what could—would—be even worse. Then God spoke to me with great compassion in His voice. He said, "Bill, you did quite well. As you know, more is yet to come, and I will continue to be with you until the very end."

CHAPTER TEN

JESUS RETURNS TO FACE TRIALS

As we started on the trip back to Jerusalem to face the enemies of Jesus, I contemplated how to ask God about the upcoming journey. "God, I know that during the trip back to Jerusalem with these madmen, Jesus will most likely be treated terribly. But I don't recall the Bible making any direct reference to it. I know there is much conjecture about what might have happened on the trip, but nothing definite. The only thing I know for sure is that Jesus was not killed like the crowd would have liked to do.

"Since I assume I am about to observe it all firsthand, can I—should I—tell people about it when I return? Assuming I do return, of course. My problem is that I can't verify how I know about it. Everything else I have experienced has biblical references. But this will not.

"I don't want people with whom I share the rest of my biblical story to challenge the validity of my source for this part. None of the Gospels refer to it, and I wonder why. It does seem to be an important element of what Jesus and I experienced. I do not want anyone to discount everything I have to share simply because there would be a missing section I cannot biblically account for. What should I do?"

God responded, "Very good point, Bill! It is something we do need to talk about. First of all, do you know what the Gospel writers' sources of information required to be included in the Bible? There were strict criteria, you know."

I said, "No, not really. Please tell me!"

God gladly continued. "Everything written by the Gospel writers, who you know were Matthew, Mark, Luke, and John, were all men I tutored. The first two I chose, Matthew and John, walked with Jesus during His entire ministry. Virtually everything they wrote they observed firsthand or was reported by Jesus or the other disciples during their many times together. Mark was a follower of Jesus but not a disciple. He was highly influenced by both Paul and Peter. Luke was not an original follower of Jesus but learned most of what He wrote from Paul and many original disciples and eyewitnesses to many events during Jesus's ministry.

"In essence, the Gospel writers either observed everything they wrote about or interviewed reliable people who were very close to Jesus and personally observed what they told the writers. Most likely, any other information would not be acceptable. In essence, no secondhand hearsay would be accepted. Most of what Matthew and John wrote was firsthand. They experienced it themselves. Much of what Luke and Mark wrote came from other sources, such as Matthew, Paul, John, and Peter."

I responded politely, "Yes, I understand that fully."

"Now, to the point at hand. None of the Gospel writers were traveling with Jesus and the mob as Jesus was taken to be interrogated. As a result, none of the Gospel writers had direct access to the facts. Second, none of the direct observers—the mob—would probably share what they did with any of the Gospel writers, and if they did, nothing they would say could be trusted. And third, none of the Gospel writers ever got to speak to Jesus again, so Jesus could not share His experience with them.

"Some Jewish historians attempted to learn more about this moment, but nothing they heard was reliable. So most people were simply left with conjecture. Of course, I know what happened, and you will find out very soon.

"So, you see, there is a very good reason for excluding this story from your retelling of these events. The decision is yours, however. You do have free will."

In response, I asked God if what I thought would be acceptable. "As you know, I observed many other events during my time with you that the Gospel writers did not include in their Gospels. What if I always qualify what I share with people when I return? I can tell them that what I share is limited to what is written in the Bible. That way, no one can claim I have attempted to add or subtract anything to or from the Bible."

God smiled, replying, "That would be an excellent alternative. Thank you. I knew I was right in trusting you with this opportunity. It's time to go. You will now find out exactly what it was like for Jesus."

The return trip to Jerusalem was far different than earlier in the evening. Even though we had no disciples, the group was much larger than it had been. Peter and John may have initially attempted to stay nearby, but they were nowhere in our sight, or more correctly, nowhere in Jesus's line of sight. Jesus's attention was elsewhere.

Jesus was no longer speaking softly and intimately to his trusted friends. Instead, He was silent as the hordes proudly touted their success in having arrested their prey without resistance from the disciples or His friends and supporters. The religious leaders had accomplished exactly what they had hoped for without going alone. The crowd found Jesus with His disciples and significantly outnumbered the small group. Judas had fulfilled his responsibility and was probably thinking about how to spend his ill-gotten reward back in Jerusalem. Very few would ever know of the change of heart that eventually led to Judas taking his own life.

The mob had found a time and place where Jesus had no public support. They encountered no opposition—other than Peter's, and Jesus Himself had quickly remedied that. Thankfully, there was no resistance from Jesus's supporters. They had all run from the scene. And possibly best of all, Jesus had not created some miraculous demonstration of His power to prevent it from running so smoothly. Instead, Jesus allowed His captors to arrest Him, bind Him, and drag Him back to Jerusalem without a word of opposition, reproach, or criticism. It could not have gone any better for the religious leaders.

The crowd acted as though they were in complete control of the situation, but I could sense from Jesus that He knew God was the only One in control. That was quite assuring for both of us, even though the trip back to Jerusalem was still difficult. Many of the temple guards took the opportunity to treat Jesus in a manner they had never considered in public. They repeatedly struck Jesus, mocked Him with insults, and blasphemed His supposed deity. Since it was quite dark, the attackers thought they would not be identified as they were attacking Jesus. Thinking they were anonymous, they would dart up to hit Jesus with a stick, rock, or fist and push Him to the ground. They would then kick Him while He was down or drag Him along the ground and then quickly return to their perceived secrecy of darkness.

Many of the voices were familiar, and I was sure Jesus knew them quite well as they shouted their insults. Despite the abuse, however, Jesus accepted what we were experiencing. We were being dragged, pulled, and pushed, little by little, back to the city. His only reaction was to pray for the ones who attacked Him, often referring to them by name. This prayerful identification only incited those who could hear Him to even greater abuse. But Jesus continued His prayers—as did I—unfazed by what they did or said.

Every so often, Jesus—and therefore I—would get a glimpse of Judas, who was taking no active role in the abuse of the procession. Instead, he played the observer, apparently trying to blend into the crowd. His facial expressions surprised me as he observed what was happening to Jesus. There was no sign of satisfaction or accomplishment. No sign of anger or resentment. If anything, there may have been a sickening look of disappointment. But disappointment in what? Hadn't this been his purpose? Hadn't he been well compensated for his betrayal? Or had Judas possibly expected some other response from Jesus, especially at the very moment of His arrest? Had he expected Jesus to resist, perhaps? To demonstrate His endless power? To start a revolution?

I would never find out what he was thinking or feeling because we would never see Judas again.

CHAPTER ELEVEN

JESUS GOES TO TRIALS AND IS FOUND GUILTY

W e did see Peter, as well as John, again that night. Jesus had been taken by the crowd directly to the houses of Annas and then Caiaphas, where Jesus was first interrogated by these Jewish religious leaders, both former and current. He remained silent in response to their demands.

Instead, He looked around at the crowd of onlookers warmed by the fire in the accompanying courtyards. Shortly after we had arrived, we saw that Peter and John had been allowed to enter the courtyard and to stand among those who came to observe. We also noticed that a significant number of other religious leaders had arrived. However, those few Jewish leaders who supported Jesus and accepted what He had preached were conspicuous in their absence. Had they been afraid to attend? Had they failed to partici-pate in protest of the actions of the majority? Another possible and probable answer, however, was that they had intentionally not been invited and knew nothing about the illegal proceedings that were taking place.

It was obvious that whatever was about to happen would be conducted unfairly. There would be no one there to speak on Jesus's behalf other than possibly John and Peter. But there was no reason to expect them to have the courage to do so!

These carefully selected religious leaders presented well-orchestrated pretenses of trials complete with false accusations, lying witnesses, and unscrupulous judges. The trials were conducted in a very efficient manner, all before sunrise, under the cloak and protection of darkness. It was clear that the leaders had decided, well in advance, that Jesus would be found guilty of blasphemy, a charge that would justify—at least in their minds—having Jesus put to death.

During His time at the homes of chief priests Annas and Caiaphas, Jesus kept a close eye on Peter, who seemed to be undergoing his interrogation by some of the bystanders. Peter immediately objected to whatever they were saying to him and erupted into a violent, loud, and profane response that was easily heard by all.

At that moment, Peter was stunned by the sound of a rooster crowing—once—and then again. It was clear from his expression that Peter suddenly remembered Jesus's prediction of three denials—which Peter had so adamantly rejected as even being a possibility, much less a prophetic fulfillment. In an instant, Peter turned and looked at Jesus, who was now looking from afar deep into Peter's eyes. Rather than immediately accepting the forgiveness that Jesus would have offered, Peter broke into tears and ran from the courtyard in apparent shame. We would not see Peter again during my time with Jesus.

It was clear from the hushed and passionate conversations we heard among the religious leaders that the charge of blasphemy against Jesus that had been presented to the chief priests would not be convincing to the Roman authorities. It would not be considered worthy of putting a man to death. Only the Romans had the authority to sentence Jesus to death, and they would need something far worse than blaspheming God, in whom they had no belief or interest.

Revising the charge from blasphemy to insurrection, the crowd proceeded to the Roman governors of Judah and Galilee. There, the religious leaders hoped to gain the support of the Roman leaders by arguing that Jesus sought to overthrow the Roman government and become king of the Roman Empire. This charge was punishable by death on the cross if proven.

As darkness turned into light, we were shuttled between Pilate and Herod as the Roman governors tried to decide who had jurisdiction over the disposition of Jesus. Treating Jesus as more of a curiosity than a threat, neither of them could find any fault with Jesus—certainly nothing that could justify death. Pilate, especially, wanted to have nothing to do with convicting Jesus and sentencing Him to death. He even washed his hands in a fearful attempt to disassociate himself from blood that might eventually be shed. This wasted and meaningless display on Pilate's part came shortly after his wife had drawn him aside and passionately conferred with him for several minutes.

It was fascinating observing Pilate as he interrogated Jesus. He seemed more interested in a discussion with Jesus than an interrogation. As he talked with Jesus, I could feel the intensity of his gaze as he looked straight into Jesus's eyes. He listened intently and respectfully to what Jesus had to say. Pilate seemed to be amazed by this simple preacher from Galilee. I got the impression that Pilate was truly impressed not only by what Jesus had to say but also by Jesus's calm presence in such an intense and hostile environment.

I believe Pilate liked, or at least respected, Jesus as a person. He might have enjoyed discussing issues with Jesus if it had been a different time and place. He did not want to harm this amazing person. He certainly did not want to have Him put to death. So Pilate sought to justify the release of Jesus using the tradition of allowing a criminal to go free based on the crowd's support. Pilate offered the crowd two choices—Barabbas or Jesus.

Pilate was seemingly surprised by the crowd's response. He must have assumed the crowd would demand Jesus's release since they had been so much in support of Jesus just a few days earlier. Instead, the crowd repeatedly demanded the release of a criminal named Barabbas. When asked what they wanted to be done with Jesus, they shouted—over and over—"Crucify Him! Crucify Him!"

It now became evident that Pilate was an extremely weak and truly political man. When the crowd kept yelling in a deafening manner that Jesus must be crucified, it seemed to intimidate Pilate greatly. Should he release Jesus—who He knew had done no wrong—or Barabbas, an already convicted insurrectionist and murderer?

As he was assaulted by the angry emotions of the crowd, which the impassioned encouragement of the Pharisees had brought on, his reasonable and somewhat pleasant expression changed instantly. I could see his eyes grow narrow and inflamed as he took his focus off Jesus and turned his attention to the throng of protestors. Satan, not Pilate, was now in control.

He no longer cared about being fair. It no longer mattered that he liked Jesus. He realized that this was a crucial moment in a political career that he had carefully developed and nurtured. He knew that to protect his career, he must prevent these lunatics from causing a disturbance that might upset the powers that be in Rome. Jesus would have to be sacrificed—that is what the crowd wanted. Jesus must be crucified—although Pilate had never found Him guilty of any offense worthy of such a punishment. Though no charges had been proved, punishment would have to be inflicted. All that mattered now was keeping the wild crowd—and Satan, happy.

Fearing a riot if he denied the crowd's consensus, Pilate quickly returned to the crowd's impassioned demands and turned Jesus over to the palace guard to fulfill their venomous request. I could almost read his last thought: *How ironic that the man found guilty of insurrection is being released while the man who is innocent of the same crime is sentenced to death!*

CHAPTER TWELVE

PRE-CRUCIFIXION TORTURE

I t was not enough for Pilate to sentence Jesus to be crucified. Pilate also demanded that Jesus first be flogged with the infamous cat-of-nine-tails whip, a punishment that alone often killed a prisoner before his crucifixion. We were led to a courtyard, away from the critical eyes of the religious leaders who would at least be unable to find joy in viewing the punishment Jesus was about to endure.

As we entered the closed space of fanatical torturers, we were thrown to the ground, falling at the feet of men too evil-looking to describe. They appeared to be prisoners themselves and seemed to become highly aroused as they saw us enter. Most of them were holding shorthanded whips, each with many strips of leather extending from the handle. Attached to the end of each leather strip were sharp pieces of metal, bone, lead, or glass, all with ragged edges. Hanging on each edge, there appeared to be pieces of dried-out bloodied skin—likely the soiled human remains from the last victim of this horrible instrument of pain.

Before the current abuses of Jesus began, God told me that my level of pain would be much less now. I already had a reasonable idea of the pain that Jesus was experiencing. God now wanted me to concentrate mainly on what Jesus was going through emotionally because of the hatred, loathing, abhorrence, and irrationality of the people making the vicious attacks. These actions represented a small taste of the wickedness of Satan, who also wanted every Christian to bear the same abuse. But thankfully, God would only allow Satan a very short rope with us who followed Jesus. It was not hard to decide which seemed worse to me—feeling Jesus's pain, or seeing what Satan would do to us if only God would allow him to.

As the door to the courtyard closed, these monsters pounced upon us, stripping Jesus of all His clothes and chaining His hands to iron rings on a pillar that supported the courtyard roof. The rings hung high above the ground, so high that Jesus could barely touch the ground with His outstretched toes.

As the demented individuals looked on with great anticipation, their eyes blazing a wild red, they screamed unintelligible utterances of delight and passion. Then each would take his turn hitting Jesus across the back with a fierce swing of the whip, causing all of the many whip tips to inflict an injury that was enough to permanently maim, if not kill, most persons. This proved that Jesus was willing to experience even more than any of us would ever experience, not just the same. Blood flew in all directions as chunks of skin, muscle, and bone spewed upon anyone standing nearby. This taste of blood and tissue on the mouths of those torturing Jesus only excited them to greater and greater heights of frenzy as they begged and demanded to be the next in turn.

Each blow would have been enough to drive Jesus to the ground—if He had not been chained to the rings attached to the wooden pillar. Each blow, therefore, drove His tattered body into the pillar, causing the bones in His chest to make horrible cracking sounds. I soon lost count of how many blows had been inflicted—10—15—20—30. I hoped Jesus would faint so that they might stop, but Jesus remained alert, taking each blow without complaint or painful cry, a response that greatly disappointed his attackers. He prayed unceasingly for the very people who were hurting Him and praised God for the strength that enabled Him to endure. Jesus's prayers drove the maniacs to a higher level of fervor. Each fanatic wanted to be the one to put Jesus to death. Everyone, however, was deeply disappointed by their failure.

Thankfully, I could not now feel all of what Jesus was feeling. I did not want to. It was hard enough dealing with the intensity of His emotional responses to the unimaginable pain. It is hard to understand and even harder to explain. It was as if two sets of emotions in Jesus were fighting each other. One was anger, resentment, rebuke, fear, doubt—all at once. But these would only last a moment. And then, as if a temptation had passed, a sense of calm, love, and sadness would replace it, and words of forgiveness, praise, and thanks would come from His lips.

I tried to imagine the pain He had to endure, but my mind was incapable of such horror. I would never suffer what He was suffering. I knew somehow that He was going through all of this so I would not have to. I then momentarily felt so helpless, so unworthy, so guilty, knowing that He would suffer like this so I would not have to.

Finally, the lashes stopped. The torturers had grown tired and lost enthusiasm. They had longed for some vocal evidence of pain, anguish, and torture to come from the mouth of their victim, but there was none. Their thirst for pleasure was not being fueled by the screams of their victim. They had grown bored, so they finally stopped. Jesus was cut down from the post, falling helplessly into the muddy pool of blood that was at His feet. The madmen were shocked—and quite disappointed—that Jesus was still alive. Most men had died from far fewer lashes from their whips. They were acting as if they had failed to fulfill their responsibilities. Little did they know that they were part of God's plan. The prophecy was clear—the Messiah would die from crucifixion—not at the hands of these whipping boys.

They called for the Roman soldiers to come and get Him, and the courtyard door was again opened. The torturers would have to remain, looking forward to their next victim, hoping he would provide them with more excitement and pleasure. The soldiers locked the door to the courtyard behind them and dragged us to a private place where they could now find their form of macabre pleasure in Jesus's suffering.

The soldiers had heard Jesus's claim to be king of the Jews while He was meeting with Pilate, so they proceeded to sarcastically honor Jesus as their king. They would bow in front of Him in extremely exaggerated motions and address Him with mocking "respect." Dressing Him in a ragged purple robe, they placed a reed in His hands and a crown on His head. They chanted repeatedly, in scornful worship, "Hail, King of the Jews."

The crown placed on the head of Jesus was made from a vine of long, stiff thorns woven into a circle of sharp spikes. To ensure that it would not fall off His head, as well as to inflict as much pain as possible, the soldiers forced the crown down upon His head as far as it would extend. Many of the thorns drove deep into Jesus's scalp, causing numerous new sources of blood to flow down His face and onto the ground. The soldiers spat upon Jesus and continued to hit Him on His head with sticks, forcing the thorns even further into His scalp. When they had finally finished with their cruel fun, they replaced the purple robe with Jesus's simple clothing and led Him out for the long walk to His death on the cross.

For quite a while, my anguish and anger had been kept at bay by Jesus's calm. It was not allowed to boil over as so many horrific acts abused Jesus. I wanted to scream out how much I hated these soldiers, the floggers, the Jewish leaders, the crowd, Pilate, Barabbas, Judas, and even the disciples. But I was not able to do so. Jesus would not let me.

Then a horrible realization came to me. What Jesus had suffered, was suffering, and would still suffer was not just at the hands of these people. I was just as guilty as they were, and here I was, judging them with such false righteousness. All the sinful things I have done and would still do in my life would be just as horrendous in the eyes of a perfect God.

The sad truth is that my sins are no different from the jagged ends of the many tails of the whips tearing skin, muscle, and bone from His body. My sins are no less offensive than the spikes of thorns that tore into Jesus's scalp. My sins are no less grievous than the acts of Barabbas, Pilate, Judas, the Roman soldiers, and the religious leaders.

Jesus, however, would not allow me to feel any grief, shame, or guilt. He let me know He had already forgiven me, so I had to forgive myself.

I then understood much more about how much appreciation and thanks I should have, need to have, and ought to give to Him every moment of my life.

Would I still feel this strongly when I returned to my everyday life? I hoped so!

CHAPTER THIRTEEN

THE LONG WALK TO THE CROSS

I t was tradition for the person being crucified to carry the very cross-beam upon which he would be nailed. The trip would wind its way along the narrow street called Via Dolorosa. For Jesus, it would be no different. He was forced to take the weight of a massive piece of olive wood upon His shoulder, which would have been challenging for any healthy man. Jesus was hardly in a condition to carry such weight, having exhausted every imaginable source of energy and strength in simply surviving the torture that had just been completed.

Jesus was joined on this walk by two other men, both of whom were also about to be crucified, both of whom also carried the instrument of their death on their shoulders. Although they appeared to have also been whipped, there were far fewer markings on their bodies and much less blood. They seemed to be much better equipped for the stamina that was now required.

As the crossbeam was placed on and tied to Jesus's shoulders, He immediately collapsed to His knees. The weight was oppressive, and Jesus's shoulders and back were covered with open flesh wounds from the lashing He had endured. Anything simply touching His wounds resulted in severe pain and shock to His system. No matter how much He tried to lift His tattered body to gain some semblance of balance and control, He continually fell back to His scarred and bloody knees. Jesus made a valiant effort to continue along the road but repeatedly fell to the ground, significantly slowing down the procession. And then He would get up.

At first, no one was there to help Him. I could be of no help as much as I wanted to. But then a man came out of the crowd and attempted to comfort Jesus. I recognized him. I believe he had been following Jesus during the last week. I recalled that his name was Simon. He tried to give Jesus something to drink and wipe His brow, but the soldiers brutally pushed him away. But seeing that Jesus was finally unable to lift the crossbeam off the ground and did not appear anywhere close to death, the soldiers demanded that Simon carry the crossbeam for Jesus.

Simon willingly came over, lifting the weight from Jesus's shoulders as he helped Jesus to His feet. From that point on, Jesus followed slowly behind Simon, who was erect as he walked through the street—at a pace slow enough to allow Jesus to stay close by. Periodically, Simon would look back at Jesus to be sure He was progressing. At first, I sensed from Simon's face that he was expressing a sense of pride at being able to do this for Jesus. But no, I was wrong. It was a sense of honor.

I could sense within Jesus a disappointment that none of His disciples were there to offer any assistance. None of His long-term followers appeared to at least show support by walking along with Jesus on the road to the cross. Most likely, the disciples' fears kept them away. And yet, just a short time ago, they swore to stay by Jesus's side no matter what happened. To be loyal to Jesus, even to their death. They had been arrogantly unwilling even to accept the possibility that they would deny or betray Jesus, as He had predicted. But where were they now? Nowhere to be seen.

Only one man, and one who had been a follower for only a short period, was willing to step out and help his Savior. Only one man, a new convert, was willing to risk his life to help Jesus. At least one man could hold his head high when this ordeal was over. The others would have to live with their guilt and shame, which Jesus had already forgiven.

As we walked along the narrow and winding street, the crowds pressed against us, making it difficult to move forward. The soldiers continually pushed the people aside, allowing us to walk along the path. Many people in the crowd had been present at Pilate's palace earlier, and several leaders attempted to get the crowd to chant the same vindictive cry, "Crucify Him! Crucify Him!" that they had screamed earlier. This time, however, they got very little support. The crowd was in a much more somber mood. There were probably those in this crowd who, like the ones nearly a week ago, had been on the road into Jerusalem. Then and now, they had no idea what was going on. They simply assumed that Jesus was just another common criminal who had violated some Roman law. There also seemed to be some people who were sympathetic to Jesus. They were very quiet as Jesus passed by, many sobbing at the prospect of Jesus's apparent fate. But where had they been when the riotous mob demanded the release of Barabbas?

Once Jesus was no longer carrying the cross, He began to peer into the crowd, looking for familiar faces to whom He would offer a blessing for their support. He even spoke directly to a group of crying women, telling them not to weep for Him but for themselves and their children. Neither they nor I had any idea what Jesus meant by that. He may have also been looking for His mother, hoping to touch her and talk to her one more time. But if not here, then surely His mother would be at Golgotha. She had to be there for Jesus!

The procession wound through the streets, down alleys, stairways, and around corners. Jesus's attention changed from looking for faces in the crowd to seeking a more distant location. Although neither of us could see very far ahead, Jesus's focus seemed to be on something that had not yet come into visual sight—on the hill where He would die. Or maybe Jesus was already focusing on what would happen after He died. After all, this hill was simply a stop on the road to His ultimate destination.

Jesus seemed to be entirely at peace as we progressed. There was no fear of what was about to happen. There was something more like a resolute apprehension of what He knew was coming and certainly did not wish to undergo.

But fear? I sensed no fear at all.

Then the soldiers forced the crowd to separate, and we stood at the bottom of a hill called Golgotha, meaning the skull. We started up the hill, where we could see three beams standing vertically in place at the top. One would hold the piece of wood that Simon was carrying. Together, they would assemble the cross on which Jesus would be crucified.

Several men held ropes, hammers, and many long nails. Soldiers had kept most of the curious crowd from the top of the hill, but several familiar and welcome faces had been allowed to climb to the top—to be with Jesus until the end. Indeed, Jesus's mother, Mary, was there along with several other women. There, too, was John, giving comfort to His mother. At least one disciple had thankfully rallied the courage to be here. It was the one man to whom Jesus could, and would, entrust the care and safety of His mother after He had died.

I sensed an incredible feeling of relief in Jesus. He would not be utterly alone in this final ordeal, at least not until the moment of His death. At that moment, even His Father would not attend. He would be without His Father for three whole days.

CHAPTER FOURTEEN

NAILED TO THE CROSS

As we stumbled to the top of the deadly skull-shaped hill of Golgotha, where so many others had been put to death, Jesus was offered a liquid that I assumed was for His thirst. After tasting it, Jesus realized it was to minimize His pain, so He rejected the whole portion. However, the two thieves who followed us drank as much as was offered. With fearful tears, they then lashed out at Jesus, cursing Him for what they perceived as arrogance in His rejection of the painkillers. Surely, they thought He would think differently about the pain once the soldiers began to pound the nails into His hands and feet. To them, He seemed—at least for the moment—not only arrogant but also a fool.

To their amazement, Jesus never minimized the pain He would experience with the gall-mixed wine offered. His unwillingness to avoid the world's pains continued to attract the vitriol and mocking of many passersby and the two rebellious thieves who hung on His left and right. It was apparent to me that Jesus was now completely at peace and fully aware of what was happening. He needed nothing artificial to get Him through this pending doom. He still had His Father with Him—at least for now. He did not want anything to disguise or minimize what He would experience for all humanity. He must face everything the religious leaders, the soldiers, the bystanders, the two thieves, and Satan had to offer and eventually defeat it all on God's terms.

Jesus was the first to be crucified. The beam that first He, and then Simon, had carried along the Via Dolorosa was placed below the vertical beam already standing erect and upright. Jesus lay on the ground with His head resting on what would become the horizontal crossbeam.

Several soldiers kneeled on top of Jesus's body to keep Him from resisting—but Jesus offered no resistance—as they placed His outstretched arms on the beam to which they would be tied. They tied His hands to the beam so they would be held in place for when the hammering of nails began. In addition, it would ensure that His weight would not cause Him to tear loose from the nails that would go through His wrists once the crossbeam was raised above the ground, causing significant weight to be shifted to His wrists suddenly.

Jesus allowed the soldiers to perform their tasks. Little did the soldiers know that Jesus would have offered no resistance to the pounding of nails, even without the ropes or soldiers holding His hands in place.

Carefully, the soldiers found the exact spot on Jesus's wrist between the intersection of several bones, where the nails would be pounded. They picked up the sharp spikes, one by one, placing them at the precise insertion spot. They raised their hammer high above their heads and swiftly brought it down with a loud grunt from the soldier. With a horrible-sounding thud and terrible force, the hammer struck the spike, which went cleanly through Jesus's wrist and slightly into the wood. The wood would take several more terrible blows to absorb each spike securely. As excruciating as the pain was, as the long nails were pounded—one forceful blow after another—it was no greater than what Jesus had already experienced and courageously endured. And once again, much to the disappointment of the audience—the soldiers, the Pharisees, and others who morbidly enjoyed such events—Jesus gave no verbal evidence of His pain. Once again, He could silently endure it by intercessory prayer.

Ropes were now tied to either end of the crossbeam, and it was raised off the ground and fitted into place on the vertical piece. Notches had been grooved out of the beam so it would fit together perfectly, requiring no nails to keep them in place.

As the cross beam came to rest abruptly on the vertical shaft, Jesus suddenly felt the full weight of His body pulling downward on His arms, pulling them out of their sockets, as the rest of His body hung limply below. Had it not been for the ropes and the placement of the nails between the bones in His wrist, surely this sudden shift of weight with the positioning of the crossbeam would have torn Jesus's hands out of the nails, sending Him back to the ground.

Only then were the ropes untied and removed, assuring that the person being crucified would experience the maximum pain for the longest possible period.

Next, Jesus's legs were tied to the vertical section of the cross, and one was laid on top of the other on a small stand that had been nailed to the vertical section. The stand was placed there so that Jesus's knees would bend slightly, allowing Him to put His weight on the stand. Without this stand, the full weight of the body would make breathing difficult, causing Him to choke to death more quickly. To assure that this would not happen, the stand allowed Jesus to lift His body upward to fill His chest with air and take a short breath before His weight would return Him to the stand—hopefully, to be able to get at least one more breath.

An innate desire to resist death from asphyxiation causes a person to instinctively continue to strive for one more breath—and another—and another. Death would only come when Jesus no longer had the strength—or the resolve—to lift his body high enough to get one more breath of life.

Because of this innate desire to live, the process would often last several days with the soldiers and an ever-dwindling crowd watching. The soon-to-be-bored soldiers probably wished that the convicted parties had died from the scourging or the long walk carrying the cross.

The Roman Empire made sure that the cross was renowned for being the ultimate tool of torture in the world. But it would not be the true source of Jesus's death. It would not determine when Jesus would die. Only Jesus would determine that.

Jesus's actions must have had a unique lifesaving impact on one of the rebellious slaves hanging on a nearby cross. He mocked Jesus along with the rest of the crowd. Near the end, however, that man ultimately chastised the other when he said, "Don't you fear God since you are under the same sentence? We are punished justly, for we are getting what our deeds deserve. But this man has done nothing wrong," Then, turning to Jesus, he added, "Jesus, remember me when You come into Your kingdom." This request prompted Jesus's loving response, "Truly I tell you, today you will be with Me in paradise."

This and only this—at least for an instant—brought us a smile and a feeling of joy.

For the next three hours, Jesus hung on the cross.

CHAPTER FIFTEEN

THE FINAL COUNTDOWN BEGINS

Once Jesus was positioned on the cross, the same steps were repeated for the two thieves at His right and left sides. Each step of their procedure, however, was met with total fear, resistance, and screams, making it all the more painful for them. Once they were raised into place, they fought violently, using up a great deal of precious strength each time they struggled to take repeated huge gasps of air. I wondered how long they could survive at their torturous pace of resistance, but fatigue soon caused them to settle down as they attempted to maximize the breaths they had remaining in their tiring lungs. Their heads, initially held in an erect demonstration of defiance, soon sagged to a bowed and defeated posture and then rested heavily on their chests. I never learned how long they had to hang on their crosses before they died.

Jesus hung on the cross with dignity. He kept His head high, never bowing to the pain, the exhaustion, or the fear that had paralyzed those to the right and left of Him. Rather than portraying a defeated foe, Jesus appeared victorious, once again in complete control. It was as if He was in defiance of those who believed that they had been the ones to orchestrate the past twelve hours. How bittersweet their joy would be. How triumphant would be that of Jesus?

Jesus, however, found no joy in being in control of His destiny. Everywhere He looked, He was reminded of the sad reason He had to be there in the first place. He looked at the soldiers as they drank their wine. They reveled in their share of booty as they divided His clothes, a partial payment for their duties that day. As time passed, they soon became bored, knowing the wait might be several days before they could take their bounty home.

Jesus looked into the eyes of the religious leaders and other bystanders as they passed in front of the crosses. They wanted to get a closer look at Jesus, smugly taking pleasure in their perceived victory. They mocked Jesus with demands that He show His power by coming down from the cross and saving Himself. Little did they know that He demonstrated His power by staying where He was. Little did they know or seem to care that if Jesus had responded to their challenge and demonstrated His power in the manner they suggested, all humanity, including possibly some of them, would have experienced ultimate and immediate defeat. There would then be no hope for the world that preceded, accompanied, or followed Him. All hope would be gone!

I was intrigued when the leaders asked Jesus for proof that He was indeed the Son of God by coming down from the cross. Yet they later ignored the proof Jesus provided when He rose from the grave—and then from the earth itself.

As they passed Jesus on Golgotha, they had to view a sign on the cross above His head. Written in all three contemporary world languages, it read, "This is the King of the Jews." Their opposition had begun several hours earlier when Jesus had been first handed over to the crowd, and Pilate demanded that the sign be nailed to the cross with Jesus. They were still arguing over it—in extreme displeasure—as they stood at the foot of the cross and looked up at Jesus. The very crime—claiming to be God—for which they had found Jesus guilty of death was now being proclaimed for all the world to see—as fact! Pilate had made sure, knowingly or unknowingly, that the world would know that this man was indeed the King of the Jews and that these religious leaders were responsible for killing their king.

This sign made me reflect on my thoughts of Pilate when he was putting Jesus on trial. Was this sign evidence that Pilate had accepted the truth of Jesus? Might that have made him the first Christian evangelist as he informed the whole world of who Pilate knew Jesus to be? Or was this act simply demeaning the religious leaders, forcing them to accept responsibility for their actions? Or had Pilate's action been controlled by God, with Pilate having no idea of its significance? Whatever the explanation, it did not matter. That small sign resulted in Jesus being glorified throughout all modern history. That small sign above the head of Jesus—placed there by the authority of Rome—proved for the world to learn later that His opponents were wrong and were being rebuked for their actions.

Jesus looked down at His mother, her close friends, and the disciple He loved the most—John. His sadness for His mother was for the sorrow that she had in her heart. He truly grieved for her. At that moment, He showed His love for her by ensuring her future. He entrusted His mother's life to John, who would become her son.

I wondered why Jesus had done this since Jesus's brothers were still alive. But then a probable answer came to me. John had been with His mother and Him here at the cross. His brothers had not. Only John could ever share this experience with Mary as they reflected on Jesus's life, ministry, and death. It was so appropriate. It also demonstrated how Jesus was still thinking clearly and lovingly. He had just taken care of a very personal task on earth as He was about to leave for eternity.

God later rewarded John, who was assigned the responsibility of informing all humanity of the nearly exact timing of and the expected earthshaking events associated with the end times of the second coming of Jesus.

Finally, Jesus looked over to the thieves on their crosses, expressing the same sorrow, compassion, and forgiveness for them. One of the two thieves continued to mock and harass Jesus, but the other one was now contrite. Was it from fear? Or was it because he had observed Jesus during the last few minutes and had come to understand Jesus's message that had escaped so many others? If the latter was the case, then he—the repentant thief—may have better understood what Jesus had to offer all humanity than all those who had heard Him speak and observed His actions for the last three years. More than His disciples, more than His family and friends.

It might have been more than the saints of the Old Testament scriptures and the believers who would come later.

This thief knew in his heart that his eternal fortune rested entirely on Jesus and that his horrible sinfulness of a lifetime could be wiped away in an instant—by this Man on the center cross. Within mere moments of death and everlasting torture, he would be saved for an eternal life of happiness. The thief made one simple request that assured them where he would spend eternity. He asked Jesus, "Remember me when You are in heaven." In response, Jesus immediately assured him that his future would be secure, that he would be with Jesus in paradise.

This thief may have appreciated what Jesus did for him more than anyone who would ever live. More, I was sure, than I had or, regretfully, ever would.

Jesus then yelled out to the Lord loud enough for people at the foot of the cross to hear. He proclaimed, "Forgive them, for they do not know what they have done." There were many responses from those listening and hearing what He said: amazement, confusion, resentment. But I realized that Jesus was more interested in the reactions of those not currently at the foot of the cross. He was looking at—and speaking to—places far beyond where He now hung. His message was for the billions more who would later sin and need His forgiveness. How would they respond?

The sun reached its full height in the sky—it was now the sixth hour—and everything went black. Although the sun was still in the sky, no light came from it. Everyone stopped what they were doing. All sounds of people moving around and talking suddenly ceased. People quietly asked each other what had happened but got no answers. As people stumbled to move about, fear set in as they tried to find a place of safety or at least a source of light. No help was coming. It was complete chaos, as people had no idea what was happening.

Within Jesus, there was no chaos, but there was horror. At that exact moment of the sixth hour, a new mental and physical sensation began in both Jesus and me. A constant pressure seemed to be forcing down on every inch of our bodies. It was as if an insurmountable weight had suddenly been placed on Jesus as He hung on the cross. But what was it that was causing this unbearable burden? How long would it last? When would it end?

Since there was no outward physical explanation, I assumed that whatever must be enveloping Jesus had come from some unexplainable place—an evil place. It was as if another world, a supernatural one beyond physical observation and experience, was causing it. Something else came to my mind, something Jesus had explained this past week from the Book of Isaiah. He told us that the following verses referred to Him.

> After he has suffered,
>> he will see the light of life and be satisfied;
> by his knowledge my righteous servant will justify many,
>> and he will bear their iniquities.
> Therefore I will give him a portion among the great,
>> and he will divide the spoils with the strong,
> because he poured out his life unto death,
>> and was numbered with the transgressors.
> For he bore the sin of many,
>> and made intercession for the transgressors.
> (Isaiah 53:11–12 NIV)

This prophecy was being fulfilled at this very moment. This weight, this burden, and this pressure on Him—and on no one else—came from all the sins of the world committed by all the people who had ever and who would ever live in this world. Past, present, and future had accumulated all the world's evil, pain, agony, and suffering. And every bit of it was being emptied into Jesus for Him to bear, poured out on Jesus like molten lava.

The weight was intolerable—but Jesus tolerated it. The burden was unjust—but Jesus justified it. The pressure was at the breaking point— but Jesus did not break. For three long hours, Jesus accepted the guilt for every rape, murder, incest, lie, theft, blasphemy, hate, anger, and unloving acts that had ever been or would ever be committed. Yet he was innocent of it all.

We are the ones who were guilty. He accepted the punishment for every single offense, although He should not have been given the punishment. He had to be exposed to, touched by, and associated with all the sins of humanity, although He was utterly perfect, pure, holy, and devoid of any sin. He was a newborn lamb that was innocent, pure, and white—now being covered with the world's garbage, feces, dirt, and decay.

I was trapped inside with nowhere to go and no way to help or escape—only to observe and feel some of what He was feeling. I knew it was just a small inkling of what He was going through. God was keeping the real pain away from me, for which I was thankful. He knew I could not have tolerated it or endured it.

I could only thank God once again for protecting me.

Another horrible realization then came to me. I no longer had the sense of security I had during the last week, knowing that I was dwelling within Jesus and always in the presence of God. That meant that this same sense of security was also gone for Jesus. God was no longer dwelling within Jesus. Jesus was now entirely on His own. He would have to bear the complete burden without God, His Father's presence, help, and strength.

He and the Father had been inseparable before the start of eternity, and they would be together throughout eternity. But now, for three horrible hours, they would be separated. The loneliness we both felt was indescribably horrific.

Why was this separation even necessary? I suppose Jesus wanted and needed to show each one of us that, as a man, He could withstand absolutely everything detestable that the evil of Satan and humanity could throw at Him. There would never be anything that we would ever experience and have to bear that had not already been faced and defeated by Jesus in human form.

I began to understand why Jesus had sweaty blood while praying in the garden last night. It certainly was not from a fear of the pain He would endure. But it may have been His disgust in knowing that He would have to experience sin, although not by His actions or fault. And knowing He would be desperately alone, separated from God through the terrible ordeal. I now understood why there was a complete absence of light that had begun at the sixth hour, and we were now experiencing. This absolute darkness was a period of separation.

It signified the absence of God. Since God is light, wherever God is, there is light. Evil always takes place in the darkness, where God is not present. That is where evil breeds and festers, out of the sight and presence of God. Since all the evil of this world was now concentrated in this one place, God would have to withdraw until it was over, leaving Jesus and me alone in the dark.

Despite the time seeming to come to a complete halt, three hours did thankfully pass for us. Jesus spoke for the first time since assuring the thief of seeing Him in paradise. Jesus quoted the Psalms, crying loudly, "My God, My God, why have you forsaken me?" He followed with a much softer request, saying, "I am thirsty," prompting a bystander to give Him a drink of sour wine. Finally, Jesus uttered a loud and determined cry, saying, "It is finished" and "Father, into your hands I commit my spirit." Jesus had taken His last breath, and then He died.

Jesus demonstrated His complete control. There would be no lingering for days on the cross. There would be no desperate efforts to get one more gasp of air. There would be no breaking of legs to quicken the process of asphyxiation. Jesus had decided it was time to give up His spirit. So it indeed finished at that very moment.

But was it?

"It is finished" meant not that Jesus had nothing left to do but that the debt of our sins was now "paid in full." The debt for our sins was paid in full by His death on the cross, but our salvation was not yet secure. Jesus had one more critical task to accomplish before He was finished. This task was the most important act—without which nothing that preceded it would have made a difference. Jesus must still defeat Satan, and He must do it on Satan's home turf.

I had spent the last week with Jesus, and I assumed my time with Him would end upon His death and that whatever I would see through Jesus's eyes would end at this time. But more was yet to come. And God also wanted me there. There was more for me to try and understand so I could fully appreciate the whole essence of His role.

We still needed to descend into a hellish place. And better yet, to break its chains!

CHAPTER SIXTEEN

DESCENT INTO HELL

In what seemed like an instant, Jesus was no longer hanging on the cross. Surprise and confusion overcame me. Where were we? Was it heaven? Definitely not! As we looked around, I knew that this could not be a place where God would want to live. There was suffering all around us. I doubted we could still be on earth; it was like nothing I had ever seen or experienced. Remembering that Scripture reported that Jesus would descend into the lower earthly regions, I concluded that must be where we were, whatever that was.

Other people were here, but they looked utterly different from anyone I had ever met. There were no looks of joy or hope on any faces. Instead, I saw only despair. They all seemed to suffer. We could hear moaning sounds from every direction. They looked at us through shallow, hollow, and disinterested eyes once they had stopped squinting, blinking, and trying to focus on seeing us. Many were entirely indifferent to our presence, but all were aware of their own. There was no doubt that they wished they were somewhere else but knew they might never be. They were restless, constantly moving from place to place as if their movement would reduce their discomfort. They seemed to be alive and dead—both at the same time. I could only think of describing them as the walking dead.

Was it simply a dream, and I would soon wake up only having imagined what I had seen, heard, and experienced with Jesus the last week? No, I didn't think so. This was very real. But it was also surreal and unreal—all at the same time. I was still with Jesus. We were not in heaven, and we were not on earth. Knowing that Jesus was without sin, how could it be hell? Besides, it was not the end times, and there was no evidence of a lake of fire.

I had this thought: *It seems like I am still inside the physical Jesus, but how could I be? Isn't Jesus in His grave now, placed there by Joseph of Arimathea? How could He also be here physically? Could we be in two places at one time? Was I now within the spirit of Jesus but not the body? Or did we only come here after Joseph placed Him in the grave? I'll have to ask God if I see Him again.*

So where exactly were we? Jesus had been burdened with all the sins of the world as He hung on the cross. Was this simply a continuation of that experience? Maybe it was somewhere between heaven, hell, and earth. Perhaps it was a place of waiting for future destinies to be determined. Maybe it was Hades where Lazarus observed the rich man in torment, seeking a drop of water. I remembered there was also a place called Sheol. Perhaps that was where we were.

All the people we passed constantly rubbed their eyes and seemed unable to see us clearly. It was as if they had been in the dark for so long that they had lost some of their eyesight. They were extremely sensitive to the bright light we brought to this place. Still, their sensitivities differed greatly, as if they had spent significantly different amounts of time since they had last experienced light. Many were attracted to Jesus, although they seemed confused about why they felt that attraction. They struggled to figure out who this stranger was as if they should somehow know the answer.

Before they could make much progress, another light appeared before us. A figure that was beautiful to the eyes and wonderfully good to behold. He appeared out of nowhere and was approaching us. He was totally unlike everything and everyone else who resided here. How could such a thing of apparent good, beauty, and joy have survived in this place? What was it? Who was he? Was it God? If it was, why was he here? There was no doubt, however, in the minds of the residents who he was. As he approached, an expression of fear replaced the indifference on the faces of the residents.

They immediately moved aside and bowed in prostrate positions as he passed through them.

His bright presence looked a great deal like the angel that appeared to Jesus in the garden to give Jesus God's support and comfort in His time of agony. But this time, Jesus showed no sign of relief or joy or approval. Instead, Jesus had a look of intense awareness and wariness, as if He were facing an enemy that He had met before; I could feel the extreme tension in Jesus and a sense of righteous anger.

Jesus addressed this man, acknowledging him simply. "Lucifer. We meet again." In the next instant, this glowing figure named Lucifer turned pitch black, except for brilliant red glowing eyes of fire. He was now so dark that we could barely see him in the otherwise lighter darkness of this place.

Satan had somehow transported himself from his kingdom on earth to this temporary place of suffering before the final judgment. Because of him, all these poor souls would likely spend eternity in a lake of fire.

His once beautiful demeanor became one of pure evil that was painful to behold. The environment changed from an uncomfortable heat to a scorching temperature. Although Jesus showed no discomfort, the residents ran to distance themselves as far as possible from this intense heat. The closer this figure came to us, the greater was the presence of horrible odors—sulfur, decay, death. He approached Jesus like a man possessed in his sense of victory, accomplishment, and satisfaction, never noticing my presence within. He began to demean Jesus with blasphemous cursing. He taunted Jesus, sarcastically demanding that he call upon God for help as if he knew that no help would be coming.

He reminded Jesus of their time in the desert. He claimed he had cleverly used the apparently failed temptations to incite Jesus to become overconfident. Lucifer said to Jesus, "I know You left our time in the desert thinking You had defeated me with Your quotes from the Bible. But remember, I had my verses to minimize the ones You quoted."

Jesus smiled and said—"Lucifer, Lucifer! You know quite well that your quotes were not from the Bible. Close, yes, but not accurate. You know you retreat with your pointy tail between your legs whenever we meet. You are wrong every time you attempt to use My word against Me. Sadly, your ignorant followers have been duped, but I—and My people—have not."

He ignored what Jesus said and took another tack. He bragged, "Jesus is now the defeated One, the One who has been rejected, found guilty, sentenced, taken to the cross, and executed by His people. Who is now the captive, the enslaved person, the possessed?"

He reminded Jesus of his time in the garden of Eden when God the Father had told the serpent that a Savior would come to crush the snake under His foot. "But who is under whose foot now?"

He then proudly proclaimed, "I am Satan, Lucifer, Beelzebub, Abaddon, Apollyon, Belial, Leviathan. Welcome to Hades, where you must call me Master. I am the only true god. I have conquered You, the son of the false god, through death. You are now my slave throughout eternity. You will go to a place of condemnation with me at the time of judgment. I am in control of Your existence from this point on. What do You have to say for Yourself, Jesus?"

Jesus said nothing and turned and walked away from him, which infuriated and confused Satan. No one walks away from him while he speaks—or so he previously believed and required. But Satan did not possess the control over Jesus he had expected. How could that be? Jesus was on his home field!

Satan demanded that Jesus turn back to him and bow down before him in praise and worship, but Jesus continued walking as if He had not heard Satan speak. Not only did this further infuriate Satan, but a sudden and sunken realization came over him. Whereas Jesus was indeed here with him, where evil, suffering, and despair reside continuously and relentlessly, Jesus was not under his control. Instead, Jesus seemed to be the One in control! How was that possible?

Satan said nothing else.

As Jesus looked back, Satan now had a look of despair that accompanied his anger and confusion. There was also an unmistakable hint of fear creeping into his distorted face. He followed Jesus at a safe distance.

During the next forty-eight hours, Jesus moved freely within this place of horror, bringing light to darkened places. He spoke to all its wretched residents, just as He had spoken to us before His death. He told them who He was, why He had come, and all He had done for them. He told them what He had told His disciples: "Do not let your hearts be troubled; believe in God and Me. In My Father's house are many dwelling places; if it were not so, I would not tell you, for I go to prepare a place for you. If I go and prepare a place for you, I will come again and receive you to Myself, so that where I am, there you may also be."

Jesus seemed to be giving these wretched souls one last chance. These were the ones who had preceded Him and Noah and had never been exposed to His message or that of the prophets. He was telling them that there was a place called heaven where He would soon be going. It was still possible for Him to prepare a place for them if they believed in Him.

It seemed like such a simple and obvious choice for them because this horrible place was just a foretaste of things that could still come for them. But wherever Jesus appealed to these poor souls, Satan was also there, putting lies into their heads just as he and his supporters did when they were on earth. As a result, nearly all their hearts remained just as hardened as they had always been. Others came very close to accepting His Word. But as they had on earth, they once again wavered and shied away from the truth, much to Satan's delight. But some—just a few—finally saw that Jesus was the genuine light and that Satan was the ruler of darkness. Despite the lies, pressure, and temptations that Satan still offered so pleasingly, these few decided to commit to Jesus. Jesus then told them that there was rejoicing in heaven at that very moment. And I could feel Jesus's joy at their conversions.

There was no rejoicing for Satan even though most had rejected Jesus. He could not stand to lose even one. Instead, Satan went into a violent and uncontrolled rage, spewing all sorts of curses toward Jesus, His Father, and the new converts. Then Satan would quickly regain his composure as Jesus went to another tortured inmate.

As Jesus lovingly proceeded from one lost soul to another, it was clear to me that each soul in this wretched place was still precious to Jesus. But each soul was also precious to Satan. Jesus would not give up on anyone despite being here in Satan's presence. And Satan would not give up on anyone, despite having Jesus in his presence.

Somehow, during this brief time with Satan, Jesus could speak with the millions that resided here. He told each one personally that no matter their choice, He would still love them. His gathering of converted souls followed with Him, protected from Satan by Jesus, as it became clear that the remaining hours were drawing short. As excited anticipation grew greater and greater for the souls who had been saved, the devastation for Satan was also increasing. He saw what was about to happen at the end of the ever-narrowing hours, which for him was pure misery.

Jesus was about to leave, taking many souls with Him from this wretched place of despair to heaven. They would join those men and women of faith in Old Testament times who had been waiting in a joyful resting place called paradise, where the thief on the cross would also be, just as Jesus had promised him.

Unfortunately, the vast majority of those living here would stay here. They would remain somewhere in the earth's bowels, with many more joining them during the next two-thousand-plus years. And on the final judgment day, they would all end up in the lake of fire. They would then live in pain and suffering throughout eternity.

Satan had won many battles but had lost the war with God the Father and now God's Son. Everything said about Jesus in Scripture had and would be fulfilled. Jesus would return to earth briefly after rising from the dead. He had defeated death, not only for Himself but for all humanity. At the end of time, Jesus would also defeat Satan in battle at a place called Armageddon, and Satan and his demons would also be thrown into a lake of fire for all eternity.

As Satan's misery compounded at the thought of this horrible defeat, he then refocused his attention and looked ahead to future battles and possible victories. He would still have the opportunity to attract billions more to his lies. Every person would have to make an individual decision as to which way they would go. To Jesus or Satan? Now, Satan would have to turn his attention to the future and forget the losses of the present.

Jesus's time in this place had quickly come and gone, and so too were the last opportunities for lost souls to be saved. They would now be doomed to spend eternity with Satan. That was devastating to Jesus. But He, too, must look ahead to every individual still on Earth and who would be on Earth in the future. Each one needed to hear the message of Jesus. Each one had to make their own choice. Each represented a new and unique battle with Satan to be undertaken by the Holy Spirit, whom Jesus would send to live in the hearts of His people. Many battles would be won, and many would be lost. There was much work to do, and it was about to begin anew.

CHAPTER SEVENTEEN

THE IN-BETWEEN

Time had passed very quickly. We had spent parts of three days with Satan and his inmates. Jesus had personally spoken to every captive who wanted time with Him. Jesus offered a final chance to countless numbers—but very few accepted His offer. My mind had drifted to a wonderful book I had read by C. S. Lewis. At one time in his life, he had been an avowed atheist who attempted to disprove the existence of God. But his efforts all turned out to be in vain. He instead became convinced of the truth of God's word—and spent the rest of his life making up for his earlier life of confusion.

His book, *The Great Divorce*, depicts large numbers of people who are bound for hell being given a second chance that would allow them to spend eternity with God in heaven rather than with Satan in hell. It was their decision and theirs alone. They were allowed to observe what could be if they accepted Christ and lived in heaven. In addition, they were reminded of the past, present, and future for them if they remained in hell.

No matter how much evidence of the glaring differences between heaven and hell was presented, most, if not all, of the inmates decided to stay where they were or would soon be. I had a great deal of trouble understanding why they would reject God's generous offer. I was reminded of a psychological condition called Stockholm syndrome, where captives of a kidnapper come to identify more with their abductor than with their family. Most of them made little effort when allowed to escape from their abusers and return to their loved ones.

When the lost are in hell, there is no love, peace, relief, happiness, hope, beauty, or joy. Yet, they decide to stay where they are. It seems that whatever reasons led them to choose hell over heaven in the first place had not changed. Whatever caused them to reject Jesus while living on earth persisted in hell. What attracts Christians to accept Christ as their Savior seems to have little appeal. Thus, most, if not all, of them accept their fate willingly. It is similar to the cases of Stockholm syndrome, where kidnappers eventually accept their captors as family and resist the opportunities to escape and return to their real family.

I forgot how long we stayed or when we left, but I was now preparing for bed with no idea where I was. Since the beginning of this week, I had wondered when I would return to the twenty-first century. From the beginning, I never asked how long I would be here. And God never told me. I guess it would be before or after our three-day visit to hell. Since we had already visited hell, we might still be in the Holy Land for quite a while. I would love to be able to stay for His resurrection, because that represents the ultimate guarantee of our promised salvation.

At this very moment, I am about to sleep, although I have no idea where I—we—happen to be. All I know is that wherever we are, it is pitch black with very little space to move around.

So where am I? The last thing I remember before we visited Satan is being taken into a very dark place where a big stone was slammed against its opening a short while later. This must have been the cave one of Jesus's supporters provided for burial.

But wait a minute! I know that Jesus died on the cross. I assume that at that moment, His human body died—and not His infinite Spirit. And it was in His human body that I accompanied Him during the last week. So how can I still be here if I was in His physical body last week, and His physical body is now dead—at least until the resurrection, that is?

And how did I travel to hell with Jesus if His body was dead? Could my memory have come from what I had learned in the Bible? No! That's not it, for I experienced much more detail than the Bible discloses about Jesus's experience in hell.

At this point, God intervened. "Bill, I have enjoyed listening to you trying to piece together all the mysteries relating to the crucifixion and resurrection. I appreciate your curiosity. Unfortunately, there are many things you will not figure out—at least not entirely or perfectly—during your finite time on earth. Only I can clarify everything for you—but only at a much later date. The Bible tells you in 1 Corinthians 13:12 that everything we see is a dim and blurry version of the real thing today. But when Jesus returns in the end times, He will reveal everything perfectly. There is no complete picture of the truth, but it is moving in a direction I think you will appreciate.

"Please tell me what you think of this partial timeline, starting with the crucifixion. God the Son, Jesus, dies in human form on the cross. He is all alone. God the Father is not with Him—or you—during these three hours. From noon to three in the afternoon, Jesus—who is entirely free of sin until that moment—is overwhelmed and tortured by all the sins of people who have and will ever live and die on earth. His death paid for all their sins, no matter when they existed on earth. And their salvation is forever based on faith, even though people who lived before Jesus only knew there would be a coming Messiah. Following the massive earthquake that greatly damaged the holy of holies, Jesus's body was taken off the cross and taken to the tomb of one of His supporters. You and His Spirit accompanied Him.

"Early on Sunday morning, and before Jesus's resurrection, the three of you visited Hell and spent some time with Satan and his prisoners. Later this morning, we returned to the tomb, awaiting the signal for Jesus, in human form, to rise from the grave—being resurrected from the dead—to meet His followers. He remained with them for forty days until He ascended into heaven, where He sits on the right side of God's throne. Both His physical and spiritual form now exist in heaven.

"Without the resurrection of Jesus in bodily form, nothing would have been enough to allow millions, perhaps billions, of followers to join God in heaven eventually. All would be lost for all eternity."

I responded in a hopeful manner. "Thank You for that explanation. I cannot wait to see the joy on the faces of His friends when they first see Him. How much longer will I be able to stay?"

"I am sorry, Bill, but I have some disappointing news—for now. You will be returning to your home in just a short while. Whether or not you get a later chance to be and walk with Jesus again will depend entirely on you. Remember when we first talked, I identified quite a few habits you had that were concerning to Me. This week, you have demonstrated an entirely different personality—almost all for the good—very good! The potential I had seen in you was consistently on display. Your potential is even better than I had hoped for.

"But—and a very big but at that!—I still need to observe you when you and I are not spiritually connected. When you return to your normal life, you will deal with all life's difficulties. I will still be with you, but you must accept that in complete faith. If you must see, hear, and talk to Me to believe or depend on Me, then that is not faith. So if I still see in you a new person—as you seem to be now—then I will allow you to see additional horizons. I will intervene and say, 'Are you ready to take a trip for the next forty days and see Jesus ascend into heaven?'

"If you are willing to embrace these terms, then we can get started on many new projects where we can continue working together. What do you say?"

I responded with joy, excitement, and appreciation. "Yes! And thank You again."

CHAPTER EIGHTEEN

THE DAY AFTER

Then—suddenly—darkness turns into light. I am aware of the sun starting to rise in the sky. My journey with Jesus is ending. I am back at home.

Despite not being present to observe it, I knew that Jesus had risen on Sunday morning. I knew that Jesus later walked the earth for forty days before He ascended into heaven to be with His Father to prepare a place for us. And I knew He would return to take us to where He had gone, to be with Him throughout eternity. However, unlike the many things I observed firsthand during the last week, I accept these future events purely on faith—a faith that is now much stronger because of this remarkable experience.

I am again in my bedroom, in the same bed as last night—or was it last week? I had prayed for God to give me more appreciation for what the Father, Jesus, and the Holy Spirit had done for me and are still doing for me. It is now the same morning that God took me back in time, two thousand years, and placed me with Jesus, allowing me to observe and experience what Jesus did during the last week of His life. I had been able to see what Jesus saw, hear what Jesus heard, and feel everything—good and bad—of what Jesus felt. I had been allowed to look at what He had done for me and all of us through His own eyes.

I am dumbfounded as I consider the reality of what God has done for me. It is far beyond any experience one could ever imagine. My time with

God was unimaginably precious. I will cherish every moment and be a totally different person.

But—and I hate saying this—I am also fearful. I fear that tomorrow, after just one day back in my everyday world, my passion will start fading. Maybe a lot. If I do not have God continuously at my side like He was this last week, how can I keep from regressing?

Suddenly, I am overwhelmed with darkness. My mind starts doing tricks on me. I start doubting everything I'd experienced as not being reality. Was everything just a dream? No, it couldn't have been—it was so real! I also met with God last night. Or did I?

I think out loud, "God, is my memory of my time with You just been part of a dream? Please tell me it was not a dream. That it was all real!"

Wow! My head is spinning! I am so confused. It seemed so real. But how can it have been? I quickly check the date on my watch. It shows the date as only one day later than when I went to bed—right here in this bed— last night. But I was gone an entire week, wasn't I? How can I share any of this with anyone else if it was only a dream? Even if it is true, why would anyone ever believe it? They'll think I am just another "Jesus freak."

Finally, a familiar voice whispers, "Such a short time home, and you are already doubting. You know what to do."

"Yes, I indeed do! And please forgive me! God, I need your help. It was real! It was!"

Then, a very strong but soft voice said, "I'm glad you turned back to Me. I knew you would. Of course, it was real! Satan is simply trying to impugn your testimony by convincing you that none of your experiences took place. Satan will give you some free time to bask in your euphoria. But after a short time—in your case, he will start almost immediately—he will try to get your enthusiasm to wane. Then, as he just did with you, he'll put doubts in your mind that it ever happened. He will try to confuse your memory. If none of this works, he will make you afraid to share your story. He'll say, 'It's not true. They won't believe you. You'll be considered a fanatic.' When you finally give up, he'll congratulate you for coming back to your senses.

"If you allow him to bring you down, He will next say something like this: 'Congratulations, you have come back to normal.' But this is a lie! It is not your normal; it is what he wants your normal to be. Therefore, it is his normal for you. You must resist."

God enthusiastically continued, "I guarantee you that every single bit of what you remember truly occurred exactly as you remember—and as you will remember for the rest of your life. I will make sure of it. Do you trust me?"

"Yes, God, I do. I am sorry for doubting."

God responded, "Yes, you may have doubted, but then you asked for My help. This is always what I want you to do. When in any doubt, turn to Me! I can tell that your trip for the week profoundly impacted you. I am so proud!"

"Thank You," I reply. "May I ask You a few more questions now that I am back to 'Your' normal? I have not used up my allotment, have I?"

"Of course not. Anything is fair game as long it involves spiritual matters. There are no winning lotto numbers, however. What would you like to know?" asked God.

"I do want to share what I have experienced. And as I promised earlier, I will limit what I share with others. I will only talk about events that are also documented in the Bible. I thank You for allowing me to see many things without biblical verification. I wondered if You would blank out those items in my mind so I could not create any controversy. You have not yet! So far, it seems You've trusted me. Thank You!"

God smiled, saying, "I am so glad you picked up on that already. Yes, I do! And will! And you are very welcome. Next question?"

"I am concerned about the next few weeks. As You know, when we first met—in person—You exposed me to who I was relative to my appreciation for You and Jesus. You raked me over the coals. And You were right. But I do have something of an excuse. I have friends who have asked me to attend Christian conferences that they claim will change my life and greatly enhance my knowledge of and appreciation for You. They told me about the weekend they spent and how their whole spiritual lifestyle had changed for the better. They pointed to their new—or renewed—Bible studies, church roles, tithing, prayer time, and relationships. I must admit it did seem very impressive—but only for a while. And only the first time I heard it.

"Many of their great intentions and activities seemed to dissipate very quickly due to expanded hours at work, more time with family and close friends, and political involvement, to name a few reasons. They seemed to embrace the same time-consuming activities they had before the conference. I asked them what happened to their new fervor. I labeled them hypocrites. Wow. It sure takes one to know one.

"You know that this week has changed me. I do have the desire to make a lot of changes in my life. But I do not want to be like them. What can I do differently?"

God responded sweetly, "That was quite a mouthful. But I do understand completely. It does bother Me as well. And there are very few people—like yourself—who take issues to heart and try to find out what has gone wrong and what must be done differently."

God continued, "Because you have asked, I will be glad to help you understand. First, do you understand what perpetual motion is?"

"I think so," I responded. "Isn't it when something is constantly moving, but nothing appears to be causing it to occur indefinitely?"

"Very good. Now let's consider the relationship between you and Me, for example," God continued. "The relationship between Christians such as you and Me, God, does not allow perpetual motion. For example, when I do something that benefits or blesses you, your response is not dictated by My action. It is only influenced. How you respond is totally up to you."

I immediately responded, "I understand."

God continued. "If I inspire a Christian conference to have a wonderful impact on you or one of your friends, I force nothing on you. I do, however, provide a spirit in you that helps you experience a wonderful energetic elation, enthusiasm, and hopefully conviction. My spirit accompanies you home and hopefully greatly influences—not causes—many significant new spiritual habits in you. However, there is no perpetual energy that guarantees you a continuous fervor into the near and distant future. That is where you come in, for your decisions dictate your actions, which can lead to a fervor and excitement that will subsequently impact your level of appreciation of Me. Only if you further feed yourself with Me can your level of appreciation be maintained or enhanced."

I said, "I think I might be finally getting this; at least, I hope so. It's pretty cool, actually, and quite logical. First, Your inspiration at the conference impacts people like me to grow significantly in spiritual maturity. Your godly boost motivates me to make important spiritual changes in my life—my time management, priorities, goals, and relationships, for example."

"Very good, so far. The tough part is next. What now?"

"Let me see. Can I think for a moment?"

"Sure. Take your time. It is quite logical."

I finally said. "Your conference inspiration and my life changes represent a cause-and-effect relationship. But—and I think this is the key—no perpetual motion assures me that it will occur in the first place nor that it will continue on its own. Instead, my current actions, which were initially the effect of attending the conference, become the subsequent cause of maintaining and enhancing my enthusiasm. I must then be sure to participate in new or repetitive activities that will stimulate me in the future. Only by realizing these cause-and-effect relationships can we maintain or enhance them through hard work and closeness to You. Otherwise, continuous swings in spiritual maturity can cause me to doubt the strength of my faith."

"That was terrific. I have to admit, I did put a few ideas in your mind to get you started. Then, I left it entirely up to you. However, it was only because of the quality of our new relationship that I had confidence you'd be able to put it all together. I could not have done much better myself! Do you see what happens when we work together? Let's keep at it."

CHAPTER NINETEEN
GOD'S FINAL WARNING

I have one more thing I would like to say. It's a warning!" God said with concern. "If you share your experience with believers or unbelievers, very few will believe you. Anyone—especially Christians—who shares an out-of-body experience is viewed with great suspicion. The same is true when one shares having gone back in time. And then, when you share all the conversations we have had, even Christians will feel awkward being with you. If these people have not experienced it firsthand, they will feel no one else could have either.

"This is not the first time I've invited people to spend time with Me. However, most decided to limit the audience they shared with their story. Those who shared their experience were often rebuked but were also blessed by those who had spiritual experiences and finally had someone else to talk to. They may not have received what they deserved here on earth for sharing, but I guarantee they will in heaven. Brave Christians who share with others will always be blessed.

"Even though you will only be agreeing with—in essence, verifying—some writings of the Bible, nothing is being added, subtracted, or changed. But some will jealously condemn you for implying you have mystical powers that others do not. Or that God had blessed you in a special, unique way—which, of course, I did—that is limited to people like yourself who now possess special privileges, powers, or superiority. As a result, you may be mocked or criticized for your honesty and bravery, but you should still be safe—which may not be true for much longer."

I struggled. "What do you mean when you say not for much longer?"

"There are many people who follow Satan, who hate you with all their being. You are dangerous in their eyes, as they attempt to have Satan be recognized worldwide as the only purveyor of truth. You will soon be considered a purveyor of disinformation who must be quieted. Do not be naive. You are now the enemy of many more people than you can imagine. They are simply biding their time until they control you—your country—and the world.

"You may even become one of the last Christian martyrs before the Rapture begins, as you face great opposition and possibly death.

"No one but the Father knows exactly when this will happen. So, hopefully, you will share what you know right now while there is still a little time left. You can make a big difference for those who do not yet know Jesus. Your story could have a wonderful impact on unbelievers. But they will have to hear, read, or maybe even see it. I can only promise you that I will be right there with you if you decide to share your story—near and far. Tell your story to everyone in your generation who will listen, and your appreciation for Jesus will be greatly enhanced and validated by others. Remember—Jesus did not die in vain!

"Today's world seeks to discredit what Jesus did for us. It is no different now from when Jesus walked the earth. You were just there in Jerusalem, so you know exactly what happened. A small group of disciples started by taking the truth of Jesus to the world outside of Jerusalem, all willing to give up their lives. As a result, new believers kept the Good News alive for the next 2000 years. Your story can have a similar impact. Who knows, it might become a popular book, then maybe a movie that reaches all around the world.

"Look at the story that is passing around from where you just returned. It is full of lies. The following story is already making its way through Jerusalem and the countryside. The same thing is happening today in your world, as the truth, significance, and wonderment of Jesus are being denied, ridiculed, and scorned. Satan will ensure it spreads even further today than he did two thousand years ago.

"The following story was the work of the evil one!"

Barabbas Released to Thunder of Support,
Local Preacher Crucified for Heresy,
Leaders Breathe a Sigh of Relief!

April 17, 0033

Jerusalem—A quite unexpected and fitting turn of events occurred this week in the city of Jerusalem. A local celebrity, Barabbas, received a last-minute stay of execution from the Roman authorities. Responding to the passionate cries of a frenzied crowd, Governor Pilate commuted the death sentence of Barabbas and sent a religious anarchist to take his place on the cross. Using the compassionate Roman tradition of annually releasing one prisoner based on popular sentiment, Pilate was pleased to release the repentant felon and turned Jesus over to the crowd to be crucified. Pilate's decision met with the unanimous approval of all those in attendance who claimed to be seeking justice. When contacted at his palace, Pilate declined to comment, but an unnamed source reported that Pilate had washed his hands of the entire affair. An elated Barabbas expressed his appreciation for finally being vindicated, saying that he knew the justice system would find truthfulness in his defense.

Jesus had become well known throughout Judea as a controversial traveling preacher. Coming from the small town of Nazareth in Galilee, he arrived on the scene nearly

three years ago with a small band of disruptive followers. Everywhere Jesus traveled, he attracted large, unruly
crowds of fanatical supporters and a great deal of opposition to his nontraditional and non-biblical messages.

Jewish leaders were persistent in their position that
Jesus was blasphemous in his claims of being the promised Messiah that had been prophesied in Scripture.
High Priest Caiaphas went even further, calling Jesus the
incarnation of evil itself because of the many supernatural tricks Jesus had performed for the people. Caiaphas
claimed that the power to perform these acts could only
have come from the devil himself.

Just one week ago, Jesus unceremoniously arrived
in Jerusalem on the back of a donkey. Sparse crowds,
indicating his fall-off of support, welcomed him as
they proclaimed him their king, throwing palms on the
already littered street as he entered the city. Soldiers were
on hand, attempting to keep the peace, but were overwhelmed. Having promoted himself as a man of peace,
Jesus displayed his violent side by brutally evicting innocent vendors from the Jewish temple. The vendors had
been graciously assisting visiting Gentile converts in the
Passover traditions. Jesus then insulted esteemed Jewish
leaders with inflammatory remarks. As a result, solemn
temple worship was disrupted, to the dismay of the Jewish
leaders, who were successfully able to restore order.

Throughout the week of Passover, Jesus continually
slinked into the temple to spew his heretical teachings to
all who would listen to him. He encouraged many naive
and gullible worshippers to reject the God-given authority
of the Jewish teachers and their inspired teachings. His
presence was credited for the divisiveness between the

Pharisees and Sadducees, who had previously been mostly agreeable about all scriptural teachings.

On the evening preceding the Jewish Sabbath and following the Passover dinner, Jesus was arrested in the garden of Gethsemane, a short distance outside the city. One of his disciples, a man named Judas, had apparently come to his senses. No longer under the spell of Jesus, Judas exposed this deceiver by directing a crowd of Jewish leaders and Roman soldiers to the place where Jesus spent each evening in prayer. With the exception of an innocent bystander having his ear violently cut off, Jesus was taken into custody without incident. None of his followers were willing to defend Jesus and fled in fear from the scene into the dark. Judas was unavailable for comment, having been hanged by the resentful followers of Jesus. He was buried with honors for his bold loyalty.

In the morning, Jesus was taken to Governor Pilate and Herod to be tried for sedition and put to death. Since Jesus had proclaimed himself to be the King of the Jews, the Jewish leaders warned Pilate and Herod that Jesus was a threat to the tranquility of the nearby Roman provinces. Although Pilate surprisingly announced earlier that he found no evidence to convict Jesus, he wisely responded to the impassioned crowd to have Jesus crucified that very day.

According to reliable sources inside the palace, Jesus was handed over to the Roman soldiers, who had Jesus interrogated and crowned as a false king. When Jesus next appeared in public, there was evidence that he had violently resisted his lawful and merciful punishment. As a result, Jesus was humanely punished.

On the way to Jesus's execution, he stubbornly refused to carry his cross, badgering a bystander named

Simon into reluctantly taking his place. Jesus then took the opportunity to arrogantly point at people in the crowd, condemning them for their supposed betrayals.

When they reached the hill of Golgotha, three crosses awaited Jesus and two other unnamed criminals. An extraordinary event occurred after the three were nailed to their respective crosses and raised into an upright position. At precisely the sixth hour, clouds made the city as dark as night, remaining for three hours. Very little of note occurred during that time, except for a loud, unidentified voice from the darkness that yelled something like "it is finished" and that he was "giving up his spirit." Suddenly, the clouds dispersed, and Jesus lay dead on the cross. Some say that Jesus somehow committed suicide, thereby cowardly avoiding any deserved suffering he was about to face. Others claimed that Jesus had faked His death to reduce any more pain.

A terrible earthquake then struck the city, lasting for several minutes. There were numerous unconfirmed reports that graves were broken open by the followers of Jesus, and spirits were released from their tombs. Jewish leaders reported severe damage to the temple, including the huge curtain that covered the temple's holy of holies being shredded to pieces from the bottom to the top. The attending priests lay dead in the outer room after being attacked by Jesus's supporters, who violated the sanctity of the holy of holies. No arrests, however, were made. Jesus's supporters continually challenged the claim that the curtain was torn from the bottom up. For some reason, they claimed that the tears went from top to bottom. No one understands why they made such a big deal of this irrelevant issue.

Once the tremors ceased, in honor of the coming Sabbath, soldiers humanely broke the legs of the other two criminals hanging on the crosses, leading to their quick asphyxiation and death. Both thieves spent their last few minutes of life yelling vile comments about Jesus.

Jesus's body was claimed by one of his affluent supporters, who placed it in a tomb the man owned. The other two criminals were claimed by no one and sent to a potter's grave. There were cries of prejudice from relatives of the two thieves about the unequal burial accommodations.

Soldiers were placed at the tomb of Jesus to prevent any malicious activities from taking place. Jesus had predicted that he would arise on the third day, and the Jewish authorities were afraid that the followers of Jesus would steal his body and claim he had been resurrected. Despite valiant efforts of the palace guard to prevent such a theft, grave robbers may have prevailed.

On the first day of the week, some claimed that the tomb in which Jesus was placed was empty when women came to complete his burial procedures. It was also claimed that Jesus appeared to his followers often during the next few days. These reports could not be verified. Attempts to get responses from Pilate and Herod were met with "no comment." However, Caiaphas did have these reconciliatory and prepared remarks: "We are sorry that this had to end up this way. We held no ill will toward this misguided man. We gave him every chance to verify if he was indeed who he claimed to be—'Lord of all.' However, he only proved to be either a liar or a lunatic, and possibly both, based on the signs attached to the cross above His head."

High Priest Caiaphas refused to comment on whether the temple curtain had been torn from top to bottom and, if true, how that could have happened, or on the earthquake and how many dead people left their tombs and appeared to spectators in the holy city. Caiaphas offered "no comment" responses as he walked away. However, he suddenly stopped and mumbled, "Maybe we'll finally get the respect we deserve again … with him gone!"

The leader of the Roman guard claimed credit for the return to normality in the city.

It is not hard to imagine a story like this coming from a secular newspaper of the twenty-first century—one full of lies, half-truths, and missing truths. Thankfully, the full truth did come out. Thankfully, those who walked with Jesus passed along an accurate version of the events. Thankfully, the Holy Spirit inspired four Gospel writers to write faithful reports of the stories they observed or learned. And thankfully, Jewish writings at the time independently validated the historical accuracy of much of the Gospel accounts.

If we of the years AD had to depend on only a modern secular version of Jesus's sacrifice, very few of us would become people of faith. There would be nothing inspiring about Jesus to follow. There would have been nobody worth dying for. World historians would have had little to write about during AD 33, except that enemies of the Roman Empire were crucified for their crimes.

But because of the Gospels and much supporting evidence from independent parties, we do know the truth. Hundreds of millions have believed that Jesus died for our sins. Millions of us know that by accepting Him as Savior and Lord—rather than liar or lunatic—we are assured of spending eternity with Him. Millions of us today call ourselves Christians.

But how many of us "card-carrying" Christians can honestly say that we truly appreciate everything Jesus has done for us? That is what this book is all about. How do we appreciate Jesus, and what do we offer as evidence? Are we willing to die in His name as each of the twelve disciples was willing to do years ago? Are we willing to follow the example of millions of people who converted from other religions to accept Jesus in their hearts, knowing that they could be persecuted and could die for their commitment to follow Jesus?

AUTHOR'S NOTE

Fifteen years ago, I attended a Christian conference that greatly challenged the reality and depth of my faith. It made me take a serious look at my relationship with Jesus. Was it real? Was I as close to Jesus as I should be—and could be?

Returning home, I continued to enjoy the euphoria of my mountaintop experience—but not for long. As weeks passed, I realized that my fervor for Jesus was dwindling bit by bit. My daily prayer time, which at first was continuous throughout each day, became sporadic. My appreciation for everything Jesus had done for me was losing intensity. My life was again becoming distracted by my work, family, and favorite activities.

I realized that I did not adequately appreciate Jesus. I wasn't even close to doing so. I needed to change! I knew God wanted me to stop taking His Son for granted. He wanted me to be so excited about my faith that I would share Him with others at every opportunity.

I turned to the Lord and asked for guidance. I needed to get out of the dark mood of guilt I was experiencing. As always, the Lord responded to my concerns. I felt led to study the Gospels, reading and rereading every-thing Jesus did during His earthly life. I started making extensive notes on the last few weeks of Jesus's life and placed the events of all four Gospels in chronological order. Doing this greatly enhanced my closeness to Jesus and my love and overall appreciation for all He had done for me.

Naturally, I wanted to share this excitement with others. But how to do it was the challenge. Although I had learned much, I realized there was little new for most serious Bible readers. Could I present this sacred story innovatively in a way that would not offend any audience? Could my journey interest old and new Bible readers alike? And would it not simply be a repeat of this well-known and miraculously true story?

To my surprise, I felt led to write a very different sort of book. It would be presented from a unique perspective. It would involve someone like myself, who had not walked very closely with the Lord and felt quite comfortable in a mediocre faith.

So that was what I did.

God gave me the vision for the book over fifteen years ago. And I believe He has completed the work at the exact right time in history. Two thousand years ago, John, one of Jesus's twelve disciples, wrote the book of Revelation and forecast events that would occur during the end of world history. One prophecy was that Israel would return to its original homeland, which was fulfilled more than two thousand years later, in 1948, when Israel became the first country dispersed worldwide to be reestablished as the same country in the exact location.

Second, it was prophesied that an event called the Rapture would occur within the same generation of Israel's return. The exact timing is unknown, but it will most likely be during our lifetime.

At this very moment in time, the earth is closer to nuclear destruction than at any time in history, and Israel is at the very center of what may soon take place. The book of Revelation says quite clearly that at a yet unknown exact date, Jesus will return in the air to collect all Christians who are alive at that time to take them to be with Him in heaven. This miracle is referred to as the Rapture.

Everyone else living on earth at that time will face up to seven years of horror, called the Tribulation. Those remaining on earth can still have the opportunity to accept Jesus as Savior. Still, very few of these new Christians will survive very long, as they will be targeted for martyrdom because they decided to accept Jesus.

This very threat of death for following Christ faces Muslims and people of other religions today. They know with great certainty that they face certain death by simply accepting Christ as their Savior. Their holy book, the Koran, is clear when it says that those committed to Allah—their God—are required to kill anyone of their faith who converts to another religion, especially Christianity. As a result, Muslims who consider conversion realize that they will become a target of death, no matter where they live.

And yet, the number of Muslims converting to Christianity is growing in astounding numbers worldwide. They know that once they make the decision for Christ, it is likely they will face death or the threat of it. Very few of us who live in America or other Christian nations realize that death may also, someday, be a possibility for us as Christians and that we can demonstrate no greater evidence of our faith than a willingness to die for Jesus.

Paul's letter to the Romans tells us this concerning our guarantee of eternal salvation: "If you declare with your mouth, 'Jesus is Lord,' and believe in your heart that God raised him from the dead, you will be saved" (Romans 10:9). I truly believe that I have met this criterion in Romans, and therefore, I believe I am saved. I have to admit, however, that until very recently, I cannot say I had also expressed my willingness to die for Jesus if necessary.

Thank you for joining me in this experience of God, allowing a person like you—or me—a unique opportunity to look through the eyes of Jesus during Jesus's last week of life on earth.

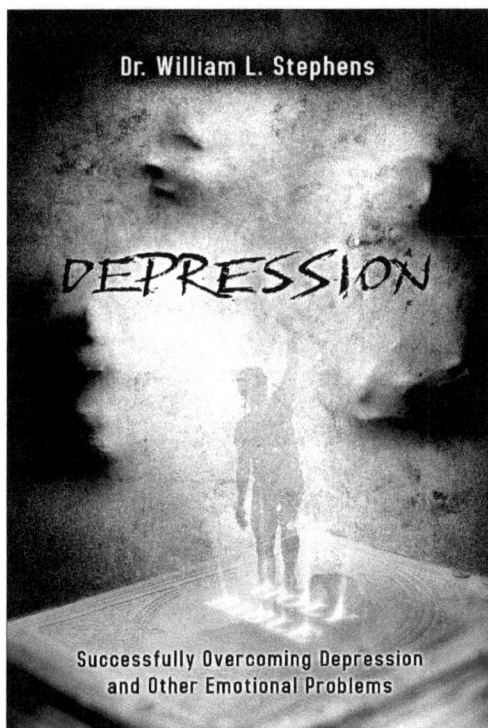

Dr. William L. Stephens

DEPRESSION

Successfully Overcoming Depression
and Other Emotional Problems

CASTLE QUAY BOOKS

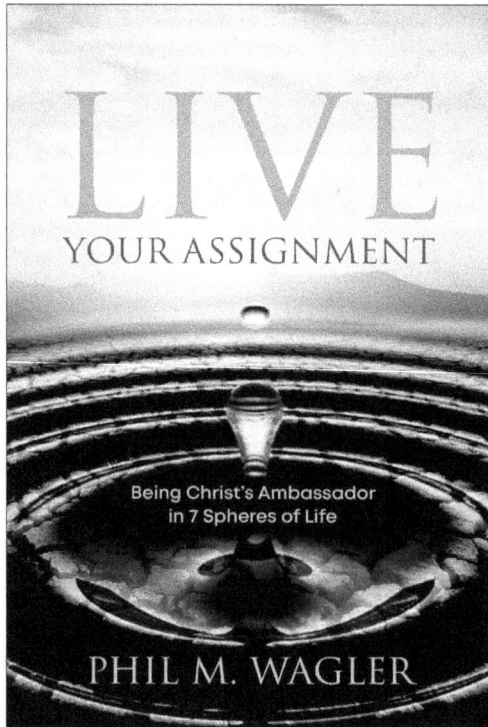

LIVE
YOUR ASSIGNMENT

Being Christ's Ambassador
in 7 Spheres of Life

PHIL M. WAGLER

CASTLE QUAY BOOKS

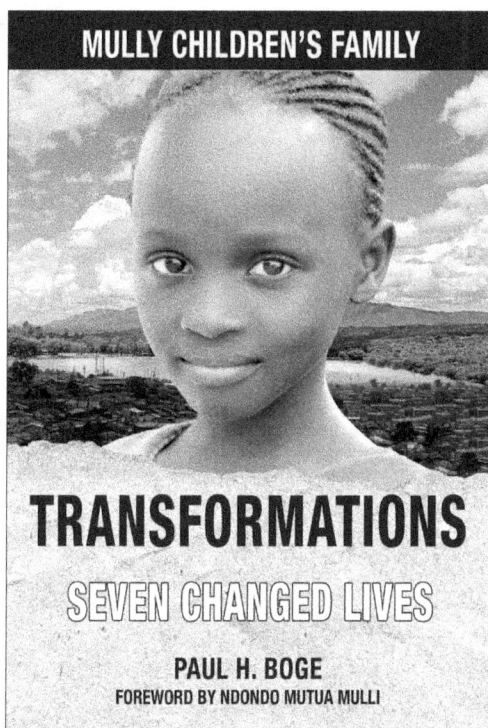

MULLY CHILDREN'S FAMILY

TRANSFORMATIONS

SEVEN CHANGED LIVES

PAUL H. BOGE
FOREWORD BY NDONDO MUTUA MULLI

CASTLE QUAY BOOKS

VIDEO SERIES INCLUDED

WOMEN
IN THE BIBLE
Small group Bible study

Winner

MARINA HOFMAN PhD

CASTLE QUAY BOOKS